FARM JOURNAL'S
COUNTRY-STYLE
MICROWAVE
COOKBOOK

FARM JOURNAL'S
COUNTRY-STYLE
MICROWAVE
COOKBOOK

104 FAVORITE FAMILY DISHES CONVERTED FOR MICROWAVE COOKERY

By the Food Editors of Farm Journal

Farm Journal, Inc., Philadelphia, Pennsylvania

Book Design: Ken Bittman
Jacket Design: Ken Bittman
Jacket Photo: William Hazzard

CONTENTS

INTRODUCTION

Whether you've just purchased your microwave oven or have been using one for years, you're probably looking for more family-style recipes with the flavor of country cooking. Over the last few years, we've received letters from both farm and city homemakers asking for home-style recipes adapted to microwave cookery, and this collection of 104 country-style dishes has been compiled with that in mind.

As you've no doubt learned, microwave cooking is a cooking adventure. Do you remember the childhood thrill of toasting a marshmallow on a stick over a campfire or barbecue grill all by yourself? Microwave cooking is just such an adventure—it's different from any other kind of cooking. It's exciting to see a cake rising in just a few minutes, scrambled eggs puffing up and ready in seconds, or vegetables cooking in plastic bags without added moisture.

When we began testing microwave recipes in our Farm Journal Test Kitchens several years ago, the entire food staff would crowd around just to watch. Many times, the microwaved dishes were even better than when cooked conventionally, although the cooking times had been slashed by as much as two-thirds. But we weren't always thrilled with the results the first time.

Some of our Farm Journal readers have been downright discouraged about their microwave ovens. For instance, a California homemaker wrote, "I'm just about to give up. My husband is not a complainer, but so far he has not liked one thing I have cooked in the microwave oven except a butternut squash. I have too much invested to use it as a planter. What can I do?"

Fortunately, other country cooks have learned through trial and error how to adapt their favorite dishes to the microwave oven, and with the recipes that follow we're sharing the benefit of their experience. In addition, we developed some recipes of our own to help you take the guesswork out of microwave cooking. All these dishes are country favorites that have been adapted to speedy microwave cooking. Before you use the recipes in this book, we suggest that you read the information and hints on microwaving in Chapter One.

Each recipe has been tested in our Farm Journal Test Kitchens and approved by our food staff home economists. We know they'll help you prepare meals quickly for your family without sacrificing the taste and eye appeal of good home cooking.

MICROWAVING: BEFORE YOU BEGIN

Microwave cooking is similar to conventional cooking in some ways and different in others. Since microwave cooking is so speedy, many traditional cooking techniques must be changed or adapted to this newer method. Before you use the recipes in this collection, we suggest you read through the pages that follow. We tell you how microwaves cook food as well as provide information on using recipes in this book in your microwave oven, special microwaving techniques, and selecting microwave utensils.

HOW MICROWAVES COOK FOOD

Microwaves are electromagnetic waves similar to radio and television waves. They are produced by a magnetron tube inside the microwave oven— this tube converts electrical energy into microwave energy for cooking. Unlike conventional cooking, where foods are cooked by heated air in the oven or a heated pan or dish on top of the range, the microwaves go directly into the food, penetrating all sides to a depth of ¾ to 1½ inches. Microwaves are absorbed by moisture molecules in the food and cause these molecules to vibrate and rub against each other at a frenzied rate. This creates friction, similar to the friction caused by rubbing your hands together, and produces heat that cooks the food.

Even when the microwaves are stopped, the friction action continues by itself, slowly tapering off. To allow for this continued cooking, many recipes indicate a standing time before the food is served. This standing time allows the "cooking" to be completed. The microwaves themselves don't accumulate in either the food or in the oven—they're just a source of heat energy.

Microwaves pass through glass, paper, plastic and wood directly to the food, but they cannot penetrate metal. For this reason, the utensils you use in the microwave oven should be carefully selected to be sure you are getting equipment that permits microwaves to pass through (see page 5 on choosing microwave utensils). Unlike conventional cooking, for instance, you can heat your coffee right in the cup or a hot dog with a bun in a paper napkin. Since the microwaves heat only the food, the cooking utensil and the air in the microwave oven remain cool. However, the food gets hot, and eventually this heats the utensil. So be careful when removing any utensil—it can get hot, especially on the bottom.

HOW TO USE THESE RECIPES

All the recipes in this book were tested in 600- to 675-watt microwave ovens. If your microwave oven has an output of less than 600 watts, you may need to use slightly longer cooking times than those specified in this cookbook. If you're not sure of the wattage output of your microwave oven, check the use and care manual or ask your dealer. If the wattage of your microwave oven is less than 600 watts, we suggest cooking the food the length of time specified in the recipe. If the food is not done, cook a little longer and check again. Since the cavity size of the microwave oven and the foods being cooked affect the cooking time, you'll need to adjust the cooking times in the recipes to suit your individual microwave oven.

Most of the recipes in this book have been tested at high setting or 100 percent power although a few of them have been tested at medium setting or 50 percent power. Since manufacturers don't have common terms for settings on microwave ovens, we've included the following chart listing some of the brands (generally top-of-the-line and new models) as a guide. If you cannot find your brand listed, consult the use and care manual from your microwave oven for settings to use.

BRAND	POWER SETTINGS	
	50% (medium)	**100% (high)**
Amana	Slo Cook	Full Power
General Electric	5/Medium or Medium	10/High or High
Litton	Simmer	High
Magic Chef	5	10
Norelco	Simmer	High
Panasonic	Medium Low or Defrost	High
Sharp	Simmer	Full Power
Tappan	Defrost or High Defrost	Normal
Toshibo	50	9 or Auto
Whirlpool	5/Medium or Medium	10/High or High

Reprinted by permission of Litton Microwave Cooking Products September 1980.

NINE MICROWAVING TECHNIQUES

Many of the techniques used in conventional cooking are used in microwaving, too—but some are unique to microwave cookery. The most common microwave techniques include:

Arranging foods in utensil. Some foods (such as chicken parts) have thick and thin sections. These uneven foods are placed with the thinner parts toward the center of the utensil and the thicker parts to the outside. This helps the thicker parts to be done at the same time as the thinner portions.

Arranging foods in microwave oven. If microwaving more than one item (such as potatoes or individual custards), arrange food or utensils in a ring pattern for more even cooking.

Shielding. Use small amounts of aluminum foil to protect sensitive areas (such as chicken wings) from overcooking. Most manufacturers now recommend small amounts of aluminum foil for shielding. However, check your use and care manual for your microwave oven before using aluminum foil, because some magnetron tubes may be affected by it.

Covering. Foods are sometimes covered to speed up cooking time, retain moisture, tenderize, cook food evenly and prevent spattering. Each recipe in this book indicates the type of cover to be used if one is needed. If recipe says "cover and microwave," use the lid that comes with the casserole. If you don't have a lid, you can substitute plastic wrap—just cover casserole tightly. You'll notice in some recipes where plastic wrap is used to cover that we suggest turning back one corner to allow some steam to escape.

Paper towels are used to wrap or cover foods (such as bacon and hot dogs in buns) to prevent spatters and absorb moisture. Waxed paper is also recommended in some recipes to hold in some heat for faster cooking and to prevent spatters. Just place waxed paper loosely on top of food or utensil. For best results, use the cover recommended in each recipe.

Rearranging. The corners or sides of utensils receive more energy than the center, so foods should often be moved around within the utensil during the microwaving process to insure even cooking. With a spoon or fork, simply move the food along the side of the utensil to the center and vice versa. If foods need to be rearranged, we indicate this in the recipe.

Stirring. Many dishes require stirring during the microwaving period. This equalizes the food temperature and shortens the cooking time. Always stir from the outside to the inside of the dish.

Turning food over. Large, dense foods, such as whole vegetables or roasts, are turned over during microwaving to prevent overcooking at the top.

Rotating. During microwaving, foods that can't be rearranged, stirred or turned over are rotated for even cooking. In our recipes, we tell you exactly how to rotate—giving dish one-quarter or one-half turn.

Letting food stand. Many microwaved foods should stand before serving. This time is needed to complete the cooking process. If the food needs to stand, this is indicated in the recipe.

TIMING IS ESSENTIAL

Time is the key to successful microwave cooking. Because micro-wave cooking is so speedy, you'll need to watch cooking times carefully. There are also some differences in cooking speeds of the various microwave oven models, so it's important to check food frequently. Always set the timer for the minimum time if there is a range of times given in the recipe. If only one time is given, check food one minute before time specified. We include a visual or physical guide to doneness for each recipe to help you decide if the food is cooked enough. Remember that microwaved foods sometimes look underdone, but standing time completes the cooking process. Overcooked foods will be tough and dry. A few recipes require a thermometer to check the internal temperature of the food for a more accurate doneness test. No special microwave thermometer is required—a standard one can be used, but may only be inserted after removing the utensil from microwave oven (as per recipe directions).

Here are some factors that can affect cooking time:

Size. Small pieces cook faster than large ones. Since microwaves penetrate foods ¾ to 1½ inches, uniform pieces under two in-ches in diameter cook from all sides.

Density of Foods. Dense foods, such as potatoes, take longer to microwave than light, porous foods like cakes and breads.

Shape. Thin parts of uneven foods cook faster than thick por-tions. Uniformly thick foods cook evenly.

Quantity. Small amounts of food cook more quickly than large amounts. In microwave cooking, time is directly related to the number of servings. When doubling a recipe, increase the time by one half and check for doneness a minute before total cooking time is completed.

Starting temperature. Room temperature foods cook faster than refrigerated or frozen foods. The cooking times in our recipes are based on the temperature at which the food is normal-ly stored.

CHOOSING MICROWAVE UTENSILS

All the recipes in this book have been tested in standard glass oven-proof dishes that are also microwave-safe—you don't need any special microwave cooking utensils. Of course, any micro-wave-safe utensils available today can be used—be sure they are the same capacity as indicated in recipe. If you're not sure if a dish is microwave-safe, you can test it easily. Place the dish in the microwave oven. Place one-half to one cup of water in a glass measuring cup inside the dish. Microwave at high setting 1 to 2 minutes. If the water becomes hot and the dish remains cool, it is suitable for microwaving. If the dish becomes hot, it is unsuitable for microwaving.

CHAPTER TWO
SPEEDY MAIN DISHES

POT ROAST IN GRAVY

1 tsp. browning for gravy
½ tsp. Worcestershire
    sauce
3 lb. eye of round beef
    roast*
1 (¾-oz.) pkg. mushroom
    gravy mix

1 (10½-oz.) can
    condensed cream of
    onion soup
1 c. water

Combine ½ tsp. of the browning for gravy and Worcestershire sauce in small cup and brush over all sides of roast.

Combine remaining ½ tsp. browning for gravy, mushroom gravy mix, onion soup and water in bowl. Spoon one third of gravy mixture into bottom of cooking bag suitable for microwave ovens. Place roast in bag on top of gravy mixture. Spread with remaining gravy mixture. Place in 12x8x2" (2-qt.) glass baking dish. Tie bag together loosely with string, leaving a space for escape of steam. (Do not use metal twist ties.) Microwave at medium setting (50 percent power) 38 minutes.

Turn roast over. Microwave at medium setting (50 percent power) 37 more minutes. Let stand in dish on wooden board or heatproof surface 20 minutes.

Remove roast from bag. Slice thinly and arrange on serving platter. Spoon some mushroom gravy over slices and pass remaining gravy. Makes 10 servings.

*Note: If your roast is a different weight, allow 25 minutes per pound. Adjust total cooking time accordingly.

CHINESE BEEF WITH VEGETABLES

1 lb. beef flank steak
1 onion, sliced
½ c. bias-cut celery
  (¼" thick)
1 tblsp. water
8 oz. fresh mushrooms,
  sliced
1 clove garlic, minced

3 tblsp. soy sauce
1½ tblsp. cornstarch
½ tsp. beef bouillon
  granules
1 (6-oz.) pkg. frozen pea
  pods
1 pt. cherry tomatoes
Hot cooked rice

Cut flank steak into 2" strips. Thinly slice meat across the grain; set aside.

Place onion, celery and water in 3-qt. glass casserole. Cover and microwave at high setting 3 minutes, or until tender.

Add beef, mushrooms, garlic, soy sauce, cornstarch and bouillon granules; mix lightly. Cover and microwave at high setting 8 minutes, or until meat loses its pink color, stirring every 3 minutes.

Add pea pods. Cover and microwave at high setting 2 minutes. Add tomatoes; stir lightly to mix. Microwave at high setting, uncovered, 2 minutes. Drain juices into glass measuring cup or dish.

Microwave juices at high setting, uncovered, 2 minutes, or until mixture bubbles, stirring after 1 minute. Stir juices into meat mixture. Serve over hot cooked rice. Makes 4 servings.

LAYERED BEEF-POTATO CASSEROLE

1 lb. ground chuck
¼ tsp. dried marjoram
leaves
¼ tsp. salt
⅛ tsp. pepper
3 medium potatoes,
pared and thinly sliced
(1 lb.)

½ c. thinly sliced onion
¼ c. finely chopped green
pepper
1 (14¾-oz.) can beef gravy

Crumble ground chuck into 2-qt. glass casserole. Cover and microwave at high setting 5 minutes, or until meat loses its pink color, stirring after 3 minutes. Pour off excess fat.

Season meat with marjoram, salt and pepper. Arrange one half of the potato slices on top of meat. Top with onion, green pepper and remaining potatoes. Pour gravy overall.

Cover and microwave at high setting 15 minutes, or until potatoes are tender, rotating dish one-quarter turn every 5 minutes. Let stand on wooden board or heatproof surface, covered, 5 minutes before serving. Makes 4 servings.

POTATO-TOPPED HAMBURGER DINNER

½ c. chopped onion
½ c. chopped celery
2 tblsp. cooking oil
1½ lb. ground chuck
1 (10-oz.) pkg. frozen peas
2 (¾-oz.) pkg. brown
  gravy mix
1 tsp. Worcestershire
  sauce

1½ tsp. salt
¼ tsp. pepper
2 c. water
Instant mashed potatoes
  for 6 servings
½ c. shredded Cheddar
  cheese (2 oz.)

Combine onion, celery and cooking oil in 2-qt. glass casserole. Microwave at high setting 4 minutes, or until tender, stirring after 2 minutes.

Crumble ground chuck into onion mixture. Cover and microwave at high setting 6 minutes, or until meat loses its pink color, stirring after 3 minutes. Pour off excess fat from meat.

Stir in frozen peas, brown gravy mix, Worcestershire sauce, salt, pepper and water. Cover and microwave at high setting 12 minutes, or until peas are tender, stirring after 6 minutes.

Meanwhile, prepare instant mashed potatoes, according to package directions. Drop 6 spoonfuls of potatoes around edge of casserole. Sprinkle with cheese.

Microwave at high setting 1 minute, or until cheese is melted. Makes 6 servings.

ITALIAN-SEASONED BEEF AND NOODLES

1 lb. ground chuck
¼ tsp. salt
⅛ tsp. pepper
1½ c. uncooked medium
  noodles
1 (15½-oz.) jar meatless
  spaghetti sauce

½ c. chopped onion
6 tblsp. grated Parmesan
  cheese
½ tsp. Italian herb
  seasoning

Crumble ground chuck into 2-qt. glass casserole. Season with salt and pepper. Arrange noodles in a layer over meat. Combine spaghetti sauce, onion, 4 tblsp. of the cheese and Italian seasoning. Pour sauce over noodles.

Cover and microwave at high setting 10 minutes, or until noodles are tender, rotating dish one-quarter turn after 5 minutes.

Skim fat from surface of mixture. Stir to break up meat. Cover and let stand on wooden board or heatproof surface 10 minutes, stirring after 5 minutes. Sprinkle with remaining 2 tblsp. cheese. Makes 4 servings.

ORIENTAL HAMBURGER WITH PEA PODS

1 lb. ground chuck
½ c. diagonally sliced
  green onions
1 (10¾-oz.) can
  condensed golden
  mushroom soup
1 (8-oz.) can sliced water
  chestnuts, drained

1 (6-oz.) pkg. frozen pea
  pods, thawed
2 tblsp. soy sauce
⅛ tsp. pepper
2 tblsp. water

Crumble ground chuck into 1½-qt. glass casserole. Add green onions. Cover and microwave at high setting 4 minutes, or until meat loses its pink color, stirring after 2 minutes.

Pour off excess fat from meat. Stir in golden mushroom soup, water chestnuts, pea pods, soy sauce, pepper and water. Cover and microwave at high setting 2 minutes, or until hot. Makes 4 servings.

GARDEN VEGETABLE DINNER

1 lb. ground chuck
¼ c. finely chopped onion
1 clove garlic, minced
½ tsp. salt
⅛ tsp. pepper
1 (8-oz.) can tomato
  sauce
1 lb. unpared zucchini,
  sliced ¼" thick (4 c.)
5 tomatoes, peeled and
  sliced

½ c. chopped green
  pepper
1 tsp. dried basil leaves
½ tsp. salt
1 tblsp. cooking oil
½ c. grated Parmesan
  cheese
2 tblsp. chopped fresh
  parsley

Crumble ground chuck into 1½-qt. glass casserole. Add onion, garlic, ½ tsp. salt and pepper. Cover and microwave at high setting 5 minutes, or until meat loses its pink color, stirring after 3 minutes.

Pour off excess fat from meat mixture. Stir in tomato sauce; set aside.

Arrange one half of the zucchini in 12x8x2" (2-qt.) glass baking dish. Top with one half of the tomatoes, all the green pepper and one half of the basil. Then top with remaining zucchini, tomatoes and basil. Sprinkle with ½ tsp. salt and oil. Cover with plastic wrap, turning back one corner to allow for escape of steam.

Microwave at high setting 20 minutes, or until vegetables are tender, rotating dish one-quarter turn every 5 minutes. Pour off juices.

Spoon meat mixture evenly over top of vegetables. Sprinkle with cheese and parsley. Cover and microwave at high setting 5 minutes, or until hot, rotating dish one-quarter turn after 3 minutes. Let stand on wooden board or heatproof surface, covered, 5 minutes before serving. Makes 6 servings.

ENCHILADA CASSEROLE

2 tblsp. butter or regular
  margarine
½ c. chopped onion
¼ c. finely chopped celery
3 (8-oz.) cans tomato
  sauce
2 tblsp. chopped fresh
  parsley
5 tsp. chili powder
1 bay leaf
⅛ tsp. pepper
1 lb. ground chuck

¼ c. chopped onion
1 (16-oz.) can refried
  beans
¼ c. taco sauce
½ tsp. salt
Dash of garlic powder
12 corn tortillas
1½ c. shredded Cheddar
  cheese (6 oz.)
⅓ c. sliced pitted ripe
  olives

Place butter in 1½-qt. glass casserole. Microwave at high setting 1 minute, or until melted. Add ½ c. onion and celery. Cover and microwave at high setting 4 minutes, or until tender. Stir in tomato sauce, parsley, chili powder, bay leaf and pepper. Cover and microwave at high setting 5 minutes. Remove bay leaf.

Crumble ground chuck into 2-qt. glass casserole. Add ¼ c. onion. Microwave at high setting 3 minutes.

Stir to break up meat. Pour off excess fat from meat. Stir in refried beans, taco sauce, salt and garlic powder; set aside.

Wrap a stack of 6 tortillas in plastic wrap. Slit plastic wrap to allow for escape of steam. Microwave at high setting 1½ minutes, or until soft. Repeat with 6 remaining tortillas.

Place a generous ¼ c. meat mixture on each tortilla and roll up. Pour half of the sauce into 12x8x2″ (2-qt.) glass baking dish. Place filled tortillas, seam side down, in sauce in baking dish. Pour remaining sauce over tortillas. Cover with waxed paper.

Microwave at high setting 9 minutes, or until hot, rotating dish one-quarter turn after 5 minutes. Sprinkle with cheese and olives. Microwave at high setting 2 minutes more, or until cheese is melted. Makes 6 servings.

MONTE VISTA TAMALE PIE

1 c. yellow corn meal
2 tsp. chili powder
1 tsp. salt
3 c. water
1 lb. ground chuck
½ c. chopped onion
¼ c. chopped green
   pepper
1 clove garlic, minced

1 (16-oz.) can tomatoes,
   cut up
1 (6-oz.) can tomato paste
½ c. sliced pitted ripe
   olives
4 tsp. chili powder
½ tsp. salt
1 c. shredded Cheddar
   cheese (4 oz.)

Combine corn meal, 2 tsp. chili powder, 1 tsp. salt and water in 12x8x2" (2-qt.) glass baking dish. Microwave at high setting 8 to 10 minutes, or until thickened, stirring every 2 minutes. Set aside.

Crumble ground chuck into 1½-qt. glass casserole. Add onion, green pepper and garlic. Cover and microwave at high setting 5 to 7 minutes, or until meat loses its pink color, stirring after 3 minutes.

Pour off excess fat from meat. Stir in tomatoes, tomato paste, olives, 4 tsp. chili powder and ½ tsp. salt. Spoon meat mixture over corn meal mixture. Sprinkle with cheese. Microwave at high setting 1 minute, or until cheese is melted. Makes 6 servings.

QUICK AND EASY CHILI

1 lb. ground chuck
½ c. chopped onion
½ c. chopped green
  pepper
1 (16-oz.) can stewed
  tomatoes
1 (15-oz.) can red kidney
  beans, drained
1 (8-oz.) can tomato
  sauce

1½ tsp. dried parsley
  flakes
1 tsp. chili powder
½ tsp. salt
¼ tsp. dried oregano
  leaves
⅛ tsp. pepper

Crumble ground chuck into 3-qt. glass casserole. Add onion and green pepper. Cover and microwave at high setting 7 minutes; or until meat loses its pink color, stirring after 4 minutes.

Pour off excess fat from meat. Stir in stewed tomatoes, kidney beans, tomato sauce, parsley flakes, chili powder, salt, oregano and pepper. Cover and microwave at high setting 10 minutes, stirring after 5 minutes. Makes 4 servings.

MEXICAN TACO CASSEROLE

1 lb. ground chuck
1 (16-oz.) can tomatoes, cut up
1 (8-oz.) can tomato sauce
½ c. sliced, pitted ripe olives

½ c. chopped onion
1 (¾-oz.) pkg. brown gravy mix
2 tsp. chili powder
1 c. shredded Cheddar cheese (4 oz.)
1½ c. taco chips

Crumble ground chuck into 2-qt. glass casserole. Add tomatoes, tomato sauce, olives, onion, brown gravy mix and chili powder. Cover and microwave at high setting 12 minutes, or until meat loses its pink color, stirring after 6 minutes.

Skim fat from meat mixture. Sprinkle with Cheddar cheese. Arrange taco chips in ring around the edge of casserole. Microwave at high setting 2 minutes, or until cheese melts. Makes 6 servings.

CRUSTLESS HAMBURGER PIZZA

1 lb. ground chuck
⅓ c. quick-cooking oats
¼ c. finely chopped onion
1 egg
½ tsp. salt
⅛ tsp. pepper
1 (8-oz.) can tomato
  sauce

1 tsp. dried oregano
  leaves
4 thin green pepper rings
1 (4-oz.) can mushroom
  stems and pieces,
  drained
½ c. shredded mozzarella
  cheese

Combine ground chuck, oats, onion, egg, salt and pepper in bowl. Combine tomato sauce and oregano in another bowl. Add one half of the tomato sauce mixture to the meat mixture. Mix lightly, but well. Pat meat mixture into 9″ glass pie plate. Top with green pepper rings. Cover with waxed paper.

Microwave at high setting 8 minutes, or until meat is firm to the touch, rotating dish one-quarter turn every 2 minutes.

Pour off excess fat from meat. Remove green pepper rings; set aside.

Spread remaining tomato sauce mixture over meat. Top with green pepper rings and mushrooms. Sprinkle with cheese. Microwave at high setting 1 minute, or until cheese is melted. Let stand on wooden board or heatproof surface 5 minutes before serving. Makes 4 servings.

BARBECUED MEAT LOAF

1½ lb. ground chuck
1 (8-oz.) can tomato
   sauce
1 c. quick-cooking oats
1 egg
½ c. finely chopped onion
1 clove garlic, minced
1½ tsp. salt

¼ tsp. pepper
⅓ c. ketchup
1 tblsp. brown sugar,
   packed
1 tblsp. prepared mustard
1 tsp. Worcestershire
   sauce

Combine ground chuck, tomato sauce, oats, egg, onion, garlic, salt and pepper in bowl. Mix lightly, but well. Pat mixture into 8x4x2½" (1½-qt.) glass loaf dish.

Microwave at high setting 8 minutes, rotating dish one-quarter turn after 4 minutes.

Pour off excess fat from meat. Blend together ketchup, brown sugar, mustard and Worcestershire sauce in small bowl. Spread over meat loaf.

Microwave at high setting 10 minutes, rotating dish one-quarter turn after 5 minutes, or until meat is firm and has reached an internal temperature of 145° to 150°. Let stand on wooden board or heatproof surface 5 minutes before serving. Makes 6 servings.

MEATBALL STROGANOFF

Meatballs (recipe follows)
2 tblsp. butter or regular
　margarine
½ c. thinly sliced onion
1 clove garlic, minced
2 tblsp. flour
1 tsp. paprika
¼ tsp. salt
⅛ tsp. pepper
1 (4-oz.) can sliced
　mushrooms

Water
1 tblsp. ketchup
2 tsp. beef bouillon
　granules
1 tsp. Worcestershire
　sauce
½ c. dairy sour cream
Hot cooked noodles
Chopped fresh parsley

Prepare Meatballs. Arrange Meatballs in 12x8x2" (2-qt.) glass baking dish. Microwave at high setting 3 minutes.

Turn Meatballs over and rearrange by moving outside Meatballs to center. Microwave 2 minutes more, or until firm. Cover with waxed paper and let stand while preparing sauce.

Place butter in 1½-qt. glass casserole. Microwave at high setting 1 minute, or until melted. Add onion and garlic. Cover and microwave 5 minutes, or until tender, stirring after 3 minutes.

Blend in flour, paprika, salt and pepper. Drain mushrooms, reserving liquid. Add enough water to mushroom liquid to make 1 c. Gradually stir into flour mixture. Blend in ketchup, bouillon granules and Worcestershire sauce. Microwave at high setting 4 minutes, or until mixture thickens, stirring after every minute.

Stir Meatballs and mushrooms into sauce. Cover and microwave at high setting 2 minutes, or until hot.

Stir some of the hot sauce into sour cream. Stir sour cream mixture back into casserole. Serve over hot cooked noodles. Garnish with parsley. Makes 4 servings.

Meatballs: Combine 1 lb. ground chuck, ½ c. milk, ½ c. soft bread crumbs, 1 egg, ¼ c. chopped onion, 1 tsp. Worcestershire sauce, ¾ tsp. salt and ⅛ tsp. pepper in bowl. Mix lightly, but well. Shape mixture into 16 meatballs.

SWEDISH MEATBALLS

1 ¼ lb. ground chuck
⅓ c. soft bread crumbs
¼ c. finely chopped onion
2 tblsp. milk
1 egg
¼ c. applesauce
1 tblsp. bottled steak
    sauce
½ tsp. salt
⅛ tsp. pepper

⅛ tsp. ground nutmeg
1 (10¾-oz.) can
    condensed cream of
    celery soup
½ c. dairy sour cream
¼ c. chopped fresh
    parsley
8 oz. noodles, cooked and
    drained
Chopped fresh parsley

Combine ground chuck, bread crumbs, onion, milk, egg, applesauce, steak sauce, salt, pepper and nutmeg in bowl. Mix lightly, but well. Shape mixture into 18 meatballs. Place meatballs in 12x8x2" (2-qt.) glass baking dish. Microwave at high setting 4 minutes.

Turn meatballs over and rearrange by moving outside meatballs to center. Microwave at high setting 3 minutes more, or until firm.

Pour drippings into measuring cup. Skim fat from drippings. Combine drippings, celery soup, sour cream and parsley. Pour over meatballs. Cover with waxed paper.

Microwave at medium setting (50 percent power) 5 minutes, or until hot. Serve over hot noodles. Garnish with parsley. Makes 6 servings.

SWEET 'N' SOUR MEATBALLS

1 lb. ground chuck
1 egg
¼ c. finely chopped onion
3 tblsp. water
1 tsp. salt
¼ tsp. pepper
¼ c. finely chopped onion
1 tblsp. butter or regular
   margarine

1 c. ketchup
2 tblsp. brown sugar,
   packed
2 tblsp. lemon juice
1 tblsp. soy sauce
Hot cooked rice

Combine ground chuck, egg, ¼ c. onion, water, salt and pepper in bowl. Mix lightly, but well. Shape mixture into 24 meatballs. Place meatballs in 12x8x2" (2-qt.) glass baking dish. Microwave at high setting 2 minutes.

Turn meatballs over and rearrange by moving outside meatballs to center of dish. Microwave at high setting 2 minutes more, or until firm. Pour off excess fat. Cover with waxed paper and let stand on wooden board or heatproof surface while preparing sauce. (Meatballs will complete cooking on standing.)

Combine ¼ c. onion and butter in 1½-qt. glass casserole. Microwave at high setting 3 minutes, or until onion is tender.

Stir in ketchup, brown sugar, lemon juice and soy sauce. Microwave at high setting 3 minutes, or until hot. Pour sauce over meatballs and serve with hot rice. Makes 4 servings.

PORK CHOPS 'N' STUFFING

½ c. finely chopped onion
½ c. finely chopped celery
3 tblsp. butter or regular
   margarine
6 c. fresh bread cubes
   (½")
2 tsp. dried parsley flakes
½ tsp. poultry seasoning

¾ c. chicken broth
6 pork chops, ½" thick
1 (10¾-oz.) can
   condensed cream of
   chicken soup
⅓ c. milk
Paprika

Place onion, celery and butter in 12x8x2" (2-qt.) glass baking dish. Cover and microwave at high setting 5 minutes, or until vegetables are tender, stirring after 3 minutes.

Stir in bread cubes, parsley flakes, poultry seasoning and chicken broth; mix well. Spread stuffing mixture in even layer in same baking dish. Arrange pork chops on top of stuffing, with meaty sides to outside of dish.

Blend together chicken soup and milk. Pour over chops and stuffing. Cover with waxed paper.

Microwave at medium setting (50 percent power) 40 minutes, or until meat next to bone has lost its pink color, rotating dish one-quarter turn after 20 minutes. Sprinkle with paprika. Makes 6 servings.

GLAZED HAM AND SWEET POTATOES

**4 sweet potatoes, pared
  and cut in eighths (2 lb.)
2 tblsp. water
¾ c. brown sugar, packed
⅓ c. butter or regular
  margarine**

**2 tblsp. raisins
1 (1-lb.) fully cooked ham
  slice**

Place sweet potatoes and water in 12x8x2" baking dish. Cover with plastic wrap turning back one corner to allow for escape of steam. Microwave at high setting 10 minutes, or until potatoes are tender, stirring after 5 minutes.

Drain sweet potatoes. Combine brown sugar and butter in 2-c. glass measuring cup. Microwave at high setting 3 minutes, or until mixture is bubbly, stirring after every minute. Stir in raisins.

Push sweet potatoes to the sides of dish. Cut ham slice into 4 pieces. Place ham in center of dish. Spoon brown sugar mixture over sweet potatoes.

Microwave at medium setting (50 percent power) 8 minutes, or until ham is hot and potatoes are glazed, stirring every 3 minutes.

Arrange ham and sweet potatoes on serving platter. Stir syrup in dish and spoon over potatoes and ham. Makes 4 servings.

HAM AND ZUCCHINI IN CHEESE SAUCE

¼ c. sliced almonds
½ c. chopped onion
½ c. chopped green
  pepper
2 tblsp. cooking oil
2 c. uncooked elbow
  macaroni
2½ c. water
½ tsp. salt
1 lb. unpared zucchini,
  thinly sliced (about 3 c.)

1 lb. fully cooked ham,
  cut into ½" cubes
2 c. shredded Cheddar
  cheese
1 (10¾-oz.) can
  condensed cream of
  mushroom soup
¾ c. milk
2 tblsp. chopped fresh
  parsley

Place almonds in 9" glass pie plate. Microwave at high setting 6 minutes, or until lightly browned, stirring every 2 minutes. Set aside.

Combine onion, green pepper and oil in 3-qt. glass casserole. Cover and microwave at high setting 5 minutes, or until vegetables are tender.

Stir in macaroni, water and salt. Cover and microwave at high setting 8 minutes.

Add zucchini. Cover and microwave at high setting 8 minutes more, or until macaroni and zucchini are tender, stirring after 4 minutes.

Stir in ham, cheese, mushroom soup, milk and parsley. Microwave at high setting 4 minutes, or until hot, stirring after 2 minutes. Sprinkle with almonds. Makes 8 servings.

GLAZED HAM WITH CORN DRESSING

4 strips bacon, diced	¼ c. chopped fresh
Butter or regular	parsley
margarine	1 (7-oz.) pkg. corn bread
½ c. chopped onion	stuffing mix
1 (8½-oz.) can	1 (3-lb.) canned ham
whole-kernel corn	⅓ c. brown sugar, packed
Water	2 tblsp. prepared mustard

Place bacon in 2-qt. glass casserole. Cover and microwave at high setting 4 minutes, or until crisp, stirring after 2 minutes.

Remove bacon and drain on paper towels.

Add enough butter to bacon drippings to make 6 tblsp. Stir in onion. Cover and microwave at high setting 3 minutes, or until tender.

Drain corn, reserving liquid. Add enough water to corn liquid to make 1¼ c. Stir corn, 1¼ c. corn liquid, bacon and parsley into onion mixture. Cover and microwave at high setting 2 minutes, or until hot.

Stir stuffing mix into corn mixture; set aside.

Cut ham into 20 slices. Stand slices, side by side, so that ham appears whole, in 12x8x2" (2-qt.) glass baking dish. Arrange stuffing between slices, leaving 2 slices between stuffing layers. Tie securely with string. Cover with plastic wrap, leaving one corner open to allow for escape of steam.

Microwave at medium setting (50 percent power) 12 minutes, rotating dish one-quarter turn after 6 minutes.

Blend together brown sugar and mustard. Spread over top and sides of ham. Microwave at high setting, uncovered, 5 to 7 minutes, or until glaze begins to bubble. Let stand on wooden board or heatproof surface 5 minutes before serving. Makes 10 servings.

PIZZA STRATA

1 (12″) loaf French bread
4 eggs
1 c. milk
¼ tsp. salt
3 drops Tabasco sauce
¼ c. grated Romano or
Parmesan cheese
1 lb. mild Italian sausage

1 (15½-oz.) jar meatless
spaghetti sauce
1 tblsp. chopped fresh
parsley
½ tsp. dried basil leaves
2 c. shredded mozzarella
cheese (8 oz.)

Cut bread in half crosswise. Split each half lengthwise, so you'll have 4 (6″) pieces. Place bread, cut side down, in 12x8x2″ (2-qt.) glass baking dish.

Beat together eggs, milk, salt and Tabasco sauce, using rotary beater. Pour over bread and let stand 15 minutes.

Turn bread cut side up and sprinkle with Romano cheese. Let stand 15 minutes, or until bread has absorbed all the egg mixture.

Remove casing from sausage. Crumble sausage into 2-qt. glass casserole. Cover and microwave at high setting 5 minutes, or until meat loses its pink color, stirring after 3 minutes. Remove sausage and drain on paper towels.

Cover bread with waxed paper. Microwave at medium setting (50 percent power) 6 minutes.

Rearrange bread by moving outside pieces to center of dish. Microwave at medium setting (50 percent power) 6 minutes more.

Spoon sausage over bread. Combine spaghetti sauce, parsley and basil in bowl. Carefully pour spaghetti sauce over sausage.

Microwave at high setting 5 minutes, or until center is set, rotating dish one-quarter turn after 3 minutes. Sprinkle with mozzarella cheese. Microwave at high setting 1 minute more, or until cheese is melted. Let stand 5 minutes on wooden board or heatproof surface before serving. Makes 4 servings.

SPAGHETTI SAUCE WITH SAUSAGE

1 c. chopped onion
2 cloves garlic, minced
2 tblsp. cooking oil
1 lb. bulk pork sausage
1 (28-oz.) can Italian-style
tomatoes, cut up
2 (6-oz.) cans tomato
paste
2 tblsp. grated Parmesan
cheese

2 tblsp. chopped fresh
parsley
1 bay leaf
1 tsp. salt
1 tsp. dried basil leaves
½ tsp. dried oregano
leaves
¼ tsp. pepper
1 c. water
Hot cooked pasta

Combine onion, garlic and oil in 3-qt. glass casserole. Cover and microwave at high setting 6 minutes, or until onion is tender, stirring after 3 minutes.

Crumble sausage into onion mixture. Cover and microwave at high setting 8 minutes, or until meat loses its pink color, stirring every 3 minutes.

Pour off excess fat from meat. Stir in remaining ingredients except pasta. Cover and microwave at high setting 20 minutes, stirring after 10 minutes. Serve over hot cooked pasta. Makes 6½ c. sauce.

CHICKEN PARMESAN

½ c. corn flake crumbs
½ c. grated Parmesan
cheese
¼ tsp. dried oregano
leaves
⅛ tsp. garlic salt
⅛ tsp. pepper
1 (3-lb.) broiler-fryer,
cut up

1 egg, beaten
1 (10¾-oz.) can
condensed golden
mushroom soup
⅓ c. milk
2 tblsp. dried parsley
flakes

Combine corn flake crumbs, cheese, oregano, garlic salt and pepper in bowl. Dip chicken pieces in egg, then roll in crumb mixture. Reserve remaining crumb mixture.

Arrange chicken in 12x8x2" (2-qt.) glass baking dish, skin side down, and meatiest parts of chicken to outside of dish. Cover with waxed paper. Microwave at high setting 8 minutes.

Turn chicken over and move outside pieces to center of dish. Cover and microwave at high setting 7 minutes more.

Combine golden mushroom soup, milk and parsley flakes in bowl; stir to blend. Pour over chicken. Cover and microwave at high setting 5 minutes, or until chicken is tender and meat near the bone is no longer pink, rotating dish one-quarter turn after 3 minutes. Sprinkle with remaining crumb mixture. Makes 4 to 6 servings.

CHICKEN WITH CHEDDAR SAUCE

½ c. finely chopped onion
2 tblsp. butter or regular
  margarine
1 (10¾-oz.) can
  condensed cream of
  chicken soup
½ c. chopped pitted ripe
  olives
¼ c. finely chopped fresh
  parsley

1 (2½-lb.) broiler-fryer,
  cut up
1 c. dairy sour cream
1 c. shredded Cheddar
  cheese (4 oz.)
2 tblsp. milk
Hot cooked rice

Combine onion and butter in 4-c. glass measuring cup. Cover with waxed paper. Microwave at high setting 4 minutes, or until onion is tender. Stir in chicken soup, olives and parsley; set aside.

Arrange chicken in 12x8x2" (2-qt.) glass baking dish, skin side down, and meatiest parts of chicken to outside of dish. Cover with waxed paper. Microwave at high setting 10 minutes.

Turn chicken over and move outside pieces to center of dish. Spoon soup mixture over chicken. Cover and microwave at high setting 8 to 10 minutes more, or until chicken is tender and meat near the bone is no longer pink.

Remove chicken and place on serving platter. Blend sour cream, cheese and milk into sauce. Microwave at high setting 2 minutes, or until cheese is melted. Stir sauce and spoon some over chicken. Serve chicken with hot rice and pass remaining sauce. Makes 4 servings.

CHICKEN WITH PARSLEY DUMPLINGS

1 (3-lb.) broiler-fryer,
 cut up
2 chicken bouillon cubes
6 whole peppercorns
2 bay leaves
2 tsp. salt
1 tsp. rubbed sage
2 c. water
1 c. thinly sliced, pared
 carrots

1 c. chopped onion
⅔ c. flour
1¼ c. cold water
1 (10-oz.) pkg. frozen peas
¼ tsp. browning for gravy
1 c. buttermilk baking
 mix
⅓ c. milk
2 tblsp. chopped fresh
 parsley

Place chicken, bouillon cubes, peppercorns, bay leaves, salt, sage and 2 c. water in 3-qt. glass casserole. Cover and microwave at high setting 10 minutes.

Stir in carrots and onion. Cover and microwave at high setting 7 minutes. Stir mixture. Cover and microwave, at high setting, 7 minutes more, or until chicken is tender and meat near the bone is no longer pink.

Remove chicken from broth. Cool slightly. Remove meat from bones and cut into pieces. Discard skin and bones. Skim fat from broth. Remove peppercorns and bay leaves.

Combine flour and 1¼ c. water in jar. Cover and shake until blended. Stir flour mixture into broth. Add chicken, peas and browning for gravy. Cover and microwave at high setting 12 minutes, or until mixture thickens, stirring every 2 minutes.

Combine baking mix, milk and parsley in bowl; mix just until blended. Drop mixture by tablespoonfuls around the edge of casserole. Cover and microwave at high setting 4 minutes, rotating dish one-quarter turn every 2 minutes. Uncover and microwave at high setting 2 minutes more, or until dumplings are puffy and no longer doughy. Makes 4 to 6 servings.

CHICKEN CACCIATORE

1 c. sliced onion
½ c. chopped green
  pepper
1 clove garlic, minced
2 tblsp. cooking oil
1 (16-oz.) can tomatoes,
  cut up and drained
1 (8-oz.) can tomato
  sauce
1 tsp. dried oregano
  leaves

1 tsp. salt
⅛ tsp. pepper
1 (3-lb.) broiler-fryer,
  cut up
8 oz. spaghetti, cooked
  and drained
1 tblsp. cornstarch
2 tblsp. cold water
2 tblsp. grated Parmesan
  cheese

Combine onion, green pepper, garlic and oil in 2-qt. glass casserole. Cover and microwave at high setting 6 minutes, or until tender, stirring after 3 minutes.

Stir in drained tomatoes, tomato sauce, oregano, salt and pepper. Cover and microwave at high setting 5 minutes, stirring after 3 minutes.

Arrange chicken in 12x8x2" (2-qt.) glass baking dish, skin side down, and meatiest parts of chicken to outside of dish. Pour tomato mixture over chicken. Cover with waxed paper. Microwave at high setting 10 minutes.

Turn chicken over and move outside pieces to center of dish. Cover and microwave at high setting 11 minutes more, or until chicken is tender and meat near the bone is no longer pink.

Arrange hot spaghetti on serving platter. Place chicken on top. Keep warm.

Skim fat from tomato sauce. Combine cornstarch and water in small bowl. Stir into tomato mixture. Microwave at high setting 2 minutes, or until mixture thickens, stirring after 1 minute. Pour sauce over chicken. Sprinkle with cheese. Makes 4 to 6 servings.

TUNA-MACARONI PIE

1 tblsp. butter or regular
  margarine
1 tblsp. flour
¼ tsp. Worcestershire
  sauce
⅛ tsp. paprika
½ c. milk
½ c. shredded Cheddar
  cheese (2 oz.)
¼ c. grated Parmesan
  cheese
1 egg, beaten
8 oz. elbow macaroni,
  cooked and drained

2 tblsp. butter or regular
  margarine
½ c. chopped onion
½ c. chopped green
  pepper
½ c. shredded, pared
  carrot
2 (7-oz.) cans tuna,
  drained and flaked
1 (10¾-oz.) can
  condensed cream of
  celery soup
¼ c. mayonnaise
Chopped fresh parsley

Place 1 tblsp. butter in 3-qt. glass casserole. Microwave at high setting 1 minute, or until melted. Blend in flour, Worcestershire sauce and paprika. Gradually stir in milk. Microwave at high setting 2 minutes, or until mixture thickens, stirring after 1 minute. Stir in Cheddar cheese and Parmesan cheese.

Microwave at high setting 30 seconds, or until cheese is melted. Stir a small amount of the hot mixture into egg. Pour egg mixture into hot mixture, blending thoroughly. Stir in macaroni.

Place 2 tblsp. butter in 1½-qt. glass casserole. Microwave at high setting 1 minute, or until melted. Add onion, green pepper and carrot. Cover; microwave at high setting 5 minutes. Stir in tuna, soup and mayonnaise. Cover; microwave at high setting 2 minutes. Press two thirds of the macaroni mixture into bottom and up sides of 10" glass pie plate. Spoon tuna mixture into macaroni shell. Spread remaining macaroni mixture over top. Cover with plastic wrap, turning back 1" to allow for escape of steam.

Microwave at high setting 7 minutes, rotating dish one-quarter turn after 4 minutes. Let stand on wooden board or heatproof surface, covered, 5 minutes before serving. Sprinkle with chopped parsley. Makes 6 servings.

COMPANY-STYLE TUNA CASSEROLE

8 oz. uncooked wide
  noodles
5 c. very hot tap water
1 tsp. salt
6 tblsp. butter or regular
  margarine
1 c. chopped onion
½ c. chopped green
  pepper
½ c. chopped celery
¼ c. chopped fresh
  parsley
6 tblsp. flour
1 (10¾-oz.) can
  condensed chicken
  broth

1 c. heavy cream
⅔ c. milk
1 (4-oz.) can mushroom
  stems and pieces
⅛ tsp. pepper
2½ c. shredded Cheddar
  cheese (10 oz.)
2 (7-oz.) cans tuna,
  drained and flaked
⅓ c. toasted, slivered
  almonds
Paprika

Combine noodles, hot water and salt in 3-qt. glass casserole. Cover and microwave at high setting 12 minutes, or until noodles are tender, stirring after 6 minutes. Rinse noodles in cold water; drain well. Set aside.

Place butter in same casserole. Microwave at high setting 2 minutes, or until melted. Stir in onion, green pepper, celery and parsley. Cover and microwave at high setting 8 minutes, or until vegetables are tender, stirring after 4 minutes.

Blend in flour. Gradually stir in chicken broth, cream, milk, undrained mushrooms and pepper. Microwave at high setting 2 minutes. Stir mixture. Microwave at high setting 6 minutes more, or until mixture thickens, stirring after every minute.

Stir in cheese. Microwave at high setting 1 minute, or until cheese is melted.

Stir in noodles and tuna. Cover and microwave at high setting 7 minutes, or until hot, stirring after 4 minutes. Sprinkle with almonds and paprika. Makes 6 servings.

SEAFOOD-RICE CASSEROLE

1 (8-oz.) can small shrimp
⅓ c. butter or regular
   margarine
1 c. chopped onion
½ c. chopped celery
1 c. uncooked regular rice
4 chicken bouillon cubes
2 c. very hot tap water

1 (6-oz.) can crabmeat,
   drained
1 c. frozen peas, thawed
1 (8-oz.) can water
   chestnuts, drained and
   sliced
2 tblsp. dry sherry

Rinse shrimp thoroughly. Place shrimp in iced water and let stand 20 minutes. Drain in colander.

Place butter in 1½-qt. glass casserole. Microwave at high setting 1 minute, or until melted. Add onion and celery. Cover and microwave at high setting 5 minutes, or until vegetables are tender.

Stir in rice, bouillon cubes and hot water. Cover and microwave at high setting 5 minutes.

Stir rice. Cover and microwave at medium setting (50 percent power) 11 to 15 minutes more, or until rice is tender. Let stand on wooden board or heatproof surface, covered, 5 minutes.

Stir in shrimp, crabmeat, peas, water chestnuts and sherry. Cover and microwave at high setting 3 minutes, or until hot. Makes 6 servings.

ASPARAGUS LUNCHEON ROLL-UPS

2 (10-oz.) pkg. frozen
  asparagus spears
¼ c. water
12 slices boiled or cooked
  ham (1 lb.)
12 slices turkey (1 lb.)
12 slices pasteurized
  process American
  cheese

1 (10¾-oz.) can
  condensed cream of
  chicken soup
2 tblsp. chopped fresh
  parsley

Place frozen blocks of asparagus in 12x8x2" (2-qt.) glass baking dish. Add water. Cover with plastic wrap, turning back one corner to allow for escape of steam. Microwave at high setting 3 minutes.

Separate thawed spears. Cover and microwave at high setting 3 minutes more.

Move outside spears to center of dish. Cover and microwave at high setting 2 minutes more, or until tender. Drain asparagus.

Top each ham slice with 1 slice of turkey, 1 slice of cheese and 2 or 3 asparagus spears. Roll up meat and cheese around asparagus and secure with a toothpick.

Arrange roll-ups in 12x8x2" (2-qt.) glass baking dish. Spread chicken soup over roll-ups. Cover with waxed paper.

Microwave at high setting 8 minutes, or until hot, rotating dish one quarter turn after 4 minutes. Sprinkle with parsley before serving. Makes 6 servings.

BACON AND EGG SCRAMBLE

8 strips bacon
½ c. chopped green
  pepper
8 eggs

1 (10¾-oz.) can
  condensed cream of
  chicken soup
⅛ tsp. pepper

Cut bacon, crosswise, into thin strips. Place bacon in 3-qt. glass casserole. Cover and microwave at high setting 6 minutes, or until crisp, stirring after 3 minutes.

Remove bacon and drain on paper towels. Pour off all but 2 tblsp. bacon drippings.

Add green pepper to drippings. Microwave at high setting 4 minutes, stirring after 2 minutes.

Beat eggs in bowl with rotary beater. Blend in chicken soup and pepper. Stir egg mixture into green pepper. Microwave at high setting 6 minutes, stirring after every minute. (Eggs should be soft and moist at the end of cooking time.) Let stand on wooden board or heatproof surface 2 minutes. Sprinkle with bacon before serving. Makes 4 servings.

——CHAPTER THREE——
QUICK SOUPS AND SANDWICHES

TURKEY CORN CHOWDER

8 strips bacon, diced
2 c. chopped onion
4 c. sliced, pared
  potatoes ($\frac{1}{8}$" thick)
1 (10¾-oz.) can
  condensed chicken
  broth
½ tsp. salt
4 c. cubed, cooked turkey
  (1")

1 (17-oz.) can whole-
  kernel corn
1 (17-oz.) can cream-style
  corn
2 c. light cream
¼ tsp. pepper
Chopped fresh parsley

Place bacon in 4-qt. glass bowl. Cover with waxed paper. Microwave at high setting 9 minutes, or until crisp, stirring every 3 minutes.

Remove bacon and drain on paper towels. Pour off all but ¼ c. drippings. Add onion to drippings. Cover with plastic wrap, turning back 1" to allow for escape of steam. Microwave at high setting 5 minutes.

Add potatoes, chicken broth and salt. Cover with plastic wrap, turning back 1" Microwave at high setting 15 minutes, stirring every 5 minutes.

Stir in turkey, undrained whole-kernel corn, cream-style corn, light cream and pepper. Cover with plastic wrap, turning back 1". Microwave at high setting 10 minutes, or until hot, stirring every 4 minutes. Ladle chowder into bowls. Garnish with bacon and parsley. Makes 3 quarts or 10 servings.

SAUSAGE-VEGETABLE CHOWDER

¾ lb. bulk pork sausage
1 c. chopped onion
½ c. chopped green
  pepper
2 c. milk
1 (16-oz.) can whole-
  kernel corn
1 (10¾-oz.) can
  condensed cream of
  potato soup

⅛ tsp. pepper
2 c. shredded Cheddar
  cheese (8 oz.)
2 tblsp. chopped fresh
  parsley

Cut pork sausage into ½" slices. Arrange sausage slices in a ring in 3-qt. glass casserole. Cover and microwave at high setting 5 minutes, or until meat loses its pink color, rotating dish one-quarter turn after 3 minutes.

Remove sausage and drain on paper towels. Pour off all but 2 tblsp. drippings. Add onion and green pepper to drippings. Cover and microwave at high setting 6 minutes, or until tender, stirring after 3 minutes.

Stir in sausage, milk, undrained corn, potato soup and pepper. Cover and microwave at high setting 9 minutes, stirring every 3 minutes. Stir in cheese. Microwave at high setting 2 minutes more, or until cheese is melted, stirring after 1 minute. Ladle into bowls and sprinkle with parsley. Makes 2 quarts or 6 servings.

LANDLUBBER'S SALMON CHOWDER

6 strips bacon, diced
½ c. chopped onion
1 (10¾-oz.) can
condensed chicken
broth
1 (5½-oz.) pkg. au gratin
potato mix
2 c. water
1 (17-oz.) can whole-
kernel corn

⅛ tsp. pepper
1 (15½-oz.) can red
sockeye salmon,
drained, boned,
skinned and broken
into chunks
1½ c. milk
⅓ c. evaporated milk

Place bacon in 3-qt. glass casserole. Cover and microwave at high setting 6 minutes, or until crisp, stirring after 3 minutes.

Remove bacon and drain on paper towels. Pour off all but 2 tblsp. bacon drippings. Add onion. Cover and microwave at high setting 2 minutes, or until tender.

Stir in chicken broth, au gratin potato mix (both potatoes and sauce mix), water, undrained corn, pepper and bacon. Cover and microwave at high setting 18 minutes, or until potatoes are tender, stirring every 6 minutes.

Stir in salmon, milk and evaporated milk. Cover and microwave at high setting 3 minutes more, or until hot. Makes 2 quarts or 8 servings.

POTATO-CLAM SOUP

6 strips bacon, diced
¾ c. chopped onion
½ c. chopped celery
2 c. cubed, pared
  potatoes (½ ")
2 chicken bouillon cubes,
  crumbled
2 c. very hot tap water

2 (6½-oz.) cans minced
  clams
2 c. milk
¼ tsp. salt
⅛ tsp. pepper
2 tblsp. minced fresh
  parsley

Place bacon in 3-qt. glass casserole. Cover and microwave at high setting 6 minutes, or until crisp, stirring after 3 minutes.

Remove bacon and drain on paper towels. Pour off all but 1 tblsp. drippings. Add onion and celery to bacon drippings. Cover and microwave at high setting 8 minutes, or until tender, stirring after 4 minutes.

Stir in bacon, potatoes, bouillon cubes and hot water. Cover and microwave at high setting 12 minutes, or until potatoes are tender, stirring after 6 minutes.

Stir in undrained clams, milk, salt and pepper. Cover and microwave at high setting 4 minutes, or until hot. Ladle into serving bowls and sprinkle with parsley. Makes 2 quarts or 8 servings.

NEW YORK CLAM CHOWDER

2 tblsp. butter or regular
  margarine
¼ c. chopped onion
¼ c. chopped celery
¼ c. chopped, pared
  carrots
1 medium potato, pared
  and finely diced

1 (16-oz.) can tomatoes,
  cut up
¾ c. water
1 tsp. salt
⅛ tsp. pepper
⅛ tsp. dried thyme leaves
1 (6½-oz.) can minced
  clams

Place butter, onion, celery, carrots and potato in 2-qt. glass casserole. Cover and microwave at high setting 7 minutes, or until tender, stirring after 4 minutes.

Add tomatoes, water, salt, pepper and thyme. Cover and microwave at high setting 12 minutes, stirring after 6 minutes.

Add undrained clams. Cover and microwave at high setting 1 minute more, or until hot. Makes 1 quart or 4 servings.

CREAM OF SEAFOOD SOUP

1 (8-oz.) can small shrimp
3 tblsp. butter or regular
    margarine
1/4 c. minced onion
3 tblsp. flour
1/2 tsp. salt
1/8 tsp. paprika
1/16 tsp. pepper
3 c. milk

1 c. heavy cream
1/2 lb. fresh or thawed
    frozen perch fillets, cut
    into 1/2" cubes
2 tblsp. dry sherry
1 tblsp. minced fresh
    parsley
Ground nutmeg

Rinse shrimp thoroughly. Place shrimp in iced water and let stand 20 minutes. Drain in colander.

Place butter in 2-qt. glass casserole. Microwave at high setting 1 minute, or until melted. Add onion; microwave at high setting 3 minutes, or until tender.

Blend in flour, salt, paprika and pepper. Gradually stir in milk and cream. Microwave at high setting 6 minutes, or until mixture thickens, stirring every 2 minutes.

Stir in perch. Microwave at high setting 2 minutes.

Stir in shrimp. Microwave at high setting 2 minutes, or until perch flakes easily. Stir in sherry and parsley. Ladle into bowls and sprinkle with nutmeg. Makes 1 1/2 quarts or 6 servings.

EASY VEGETABLE SOUP

½ lb. ground beef
½ c. chopped onion
½ c. sliced, pared carrots
½ c. sliced celery
1 small clove garlic, minced
2 tblsp. uncooked regular rice
1 (16-oz.) can stewed tomatoes

1 (8-oz.) can red kidney beans
2¼ c. water
2 beef bouillon cubes
1½ tsp. dried parsley flakes
½ tsp. salt
⅛ tsp. dried basil leaves
Dash of pepper
½ c. frozen green beans

Crumble ground beef into 3-qt. glass casserole. Cover and microwave at high setting 4 minutes, or until meat loses its pink color, stirring after 2 minutes.

Add remaining ingredients except green beans. Cover and microwave at high setting 25 minutes, or until vegetables are tender, stirring every 5 minutes.

Add green beans. Cover and microwave at high setting 10 minutes more, or until beans are tender, stirring after 5 minutes. Let stand on wooden board or heatproof surface 5 minutes before serving. Makes 3 quarts or 12 servings.

GARDEN VEGETABLE SOUP

¾ c. cut-up green beans
  (1″ pieces)
¾ c. shredded cabbage
¼ c. thinly sliced, pared
  carrots
¾ c. thinly sliced,
  unpared zucchini
1 small tomato, cut into
  8 wedges
2 oz. fresh mushrooms,
  sliced
2 tblsp. chopped fresh
  parsley
2 tblsp. sliced green
  onions

1 qt. chicken broth
¼ tsp. dried basil leaves
¼ tsp. dried marjoram
  leaves
¼ tsp. celery seed
1 small clove garlic,
  minced
3 whole peppercorns
¼ medium bay leaf
½ c. dairy sour cream
2 tblsp. sliced green
  onion tops

Combine green beans, cabbage, carrots, zucchini, tomato, mushrooms, parsley, 2 tblsp. green onions, chicken broth, basil, marjoram, celery seed and garlic in 3-qt. glass casserole.

Tie peppercorns and bay leaf in a piece of cheesecloth. Add cheesecloth bag to casserole. Cover and microwave at high setting 40 minutes, or until vegetables are tender, stirring after 20 minutes. Let stand, covered, on wooden board or heatproof surface 10 minutes. Remove cheesecloth bag. Ladle soup into individual soup bowls. Top each serving with a dollop of sour cream and garnish with 2 tblsp. green onion tops. Makes 1 quart or 4 servings.

HERBED TOMATO SOUP

½ c. chopped onion
½ c. chopped celery
2 tblsp. butter or regular
  margarine
1 (16-oz.) can tomatoes,
  cut up
1 (13¾-oz.) can chicken
  broth

½ tsp. dried basil leaves
½ tsp. paprika
½ tsp. salt
¼ tsp. pepper
1 bay leaf
2 tblsp. chopped fresh
  parsley

Place onion, celery and butter in 3-qt. glass casserole. Cover and microwave at high setting 5 to 7 minutes, or until tender, stirring after 3 minutes.

Add tomatoes, chicken broth, basil, paprika, salt, pepper and bay leaf. Cover and microwave at high setting 8 minutes, or until mixture comes to a boil, stirring after 4 minutes.

Remove bay leaf. Pour half of tomato mixture into blender; purée until smooth. Pour into bowl. Repeat with remaining half.

Return both portions to casserole. Cover and microwave at high setting 1½ minutes, or until mixture just comes to a boil. Ladle into bowls and sprinkle with parsley. Makes 1 quart or 4 servings.

BUSY-DAY SPINACH SOUP

1 (10-oz.) pkg. frozen chopped spinach	1 tblsp. grated onion
3 c. milk	1½ tblsp. flour
2 tblsp. butter or regular margarine	1 tblsp. chicken bouillon granules
	¼ tsp. salt

Place frozen spinach in 2-qt. glass casserole. Cover and microwave at high setting 7 minutes, or until tender, rotating dish one-quarter turn after 4 minutes.

Combine spinach and its liquid with 1 c. of the milk in blender. Purée until smooth.

Place butter and onion in same casserole. Microwave at high setting 1 minute, or until butter is melted.

Stir in flour. Slowly stir in remaining 2 c. milk. Add puréed spinach mixture, bouillon granules and salt. Microwave at high setting 8 minutes, or until mixture comes to a boil and thickens, stirring every 2 minutes. Makes 1 quart or 4 servings.

SPLIT PEA SOUP

**1 lb. dried split peas,
rinsed and drained
1 lb. meaty, smoked pork
hocks
1 c. chopped onion
1 c. sliced, pared carrots**

**½ c. sliced celery
2 qt. water
2 tsp. salt
½ tsp. dried marjoram
leaves
¼ tsp. pepper**

Combine all ingredients in 5-qt. glass casserole. Cover and microwave at high setting 50 minutes, or until pork is tender, stirring every 10 minutes.

Remove pork hocks. Remove meat from bones. Cut meat in bite-size pieces and return to soup. Cover and microwave at high setting 30 minutes, stirring every 10 minutes. Makes 3 quarts or 12 servings.

FRENCH ONION SOUP

4 c. thinly sliced onion
¼ c. butter or regular
  margarine
¼ tsp. sugar
¹/₁₆ tsp. pepper
Water
1 (10½-oz.) can
  condensed beef broth
5 beef bouillon cubes,
  crumbled

¹/₈ tsp. browning for gravy
¼ c. dry sherry
4 slices French bread,
  toasted
1 c. shredded Swiss
  cheese (4 oz.)
4 tblsp. grated Parmesan
  cheese

Combine onion, butter, sugar and pepper in 3-qt. glass casserole. Cover and microwave at high setting 25 minutes, or until onion is tender, stirring after 12 minutes.

Add enough water to beef broth to make 3 c. Pour over onions. Stir in bouillon cubes and browning for gravy. Microwave at high setting 6 minutes, or until hot, stirring after 3 minutes.

Stir in sherry. Ladle soup into 4 individual microwave-safe (10-oz.) casseroles. Place a slice of toasted French bread on top of each. Sprinkle each with Swiss and Parmesan cheese. Arrange casseroles in ring in microwave oven. Microwave at high setting 2 minutes.

Rearrange casseroles. Microwave at high setting 2 minutes more. Rearrange casseroles. Microwave at high setting 1 minute, or until cheese is melted. Makes 1 quart or 4 servings.

CANADIAN CHEESE SOUP

¼ c. butter or regular
  margarine
½ c. finely chopped onion
½ c. finely chopped,
  pared carrot
½ c. finely chopped celery
¼ c. flour
2 (13¾-oz.) cans chicken
  broth

1 qt. milk
1 c. shredded Cheddar
  cheese (4 oz.)
⅛ tsp. pepper
1 tblsp. dried parsley
  flakes

Place butter in 3-qt. glass casserole. Microwave at high setting 30 seconds, or until melted. Add onion, carrot and celery. Cover and microwave at high setting 12 minutes, or until vegetables are tender, stirring every 3 minutes.

Stir in flour. Blend in a small amount of chicken broth, then gradually add remaining broth and milk. Cover and microwave at high setting 18 to 19 minutes, or until mixture comes to a boil, stirring every 6 minutes.

Add cheese, pepper and parsley flakes. Microwave at high setting 3 minutes more, or until cheese is melted, stirring after 1½ minutes. Makes 2 quarts or 8 servings.

BARBECUED BEEF SANDWICHES

1½ lb. ground chuck
1 c. chopped onion
1 c. chopped green
  pepper
1 (15-oz.) can tomato
  sauce
1 (6-oz.) can tomato paste
3 tblsp. cider vinegar

2 tblsp. brown sugar,
  packed
2 tblsp. Worcestershire
  sauce
¼ tsp. salt
⅛ tsp. pepper
12 hamburger buns, split

Crumble ground chuck into 2-qt. glass casserole. Add onion and green pepper. Microwave at high setting 8 minutes, or until meat loses its pink color, stirring every 3 minutes.

Pour off excess fat from meat. Stir in tomato sauce, tomato paste, vinegar, brown sugar, Worcestershire sauce, salt and pepper.

Cover and microwave at high setting 10 minutes, stirring every 3 minutes. Let stand on wooden board or heatproof surface, covered, 10 minutes.

Spoon meat mixture onto bottom half of hamburger buns, using about ⅓ c. per bun. Cover with top half of buns. Makes 12 sandwiches.

TACO BURGERS

1 lb. ground beef
½ c. chopped onion
1 clove garlic, minced
1 (8-oz.) can tomato
  sauce
1 tblsp. chili powder

½ tsp. salt
6 hamburger buns, split
6 lettuce leaves
¾ c. shredded Cheddar
  cheese (3 oz.)
Taco sauce

Crumble ground beef in 2-qt. glass casserole. Add onion and garlic. Cover and microwave at high setting 4 minutes, or until meat loses its pink color, stirring after 2 minutes.

Pour off excess fat from meat. Stir in tomato sauce, chili powder and salt. Cover and microwave at high setting 5 minutes, stirring after 3 minutes.

Arrange hamburger buns in ring on paper plate. Cover with paper towel. Microwave at high setting 1 minute.

Place a lettuce leaf on bottom half of each bun. Top each with ⅓ c. of the meat mixture. Then sprinkle each with 2 tblsp. of the cheese and top with bun half. Serve with taco sauce. Makes 6 sandwiches.

MICROWAVE REUBEN SANDWICHES

8 slices rye bread, toasted
2 tblsp. Russian or
  Thousand Island salad
  dressing
4 oz. sliced corned beef

1 (8-oz.) can sauerkraut,
  drained
4 oz. sliced Swiss cheese
Butter or regular
  margarine

Line a 12x8x2" (2-qt.) glass baking dish with paper towels.

Spread 4 slices toasted bread with Russian dressing. Place bread in prepared baking dish. Top each with one fourth of the corned beef, one fourth of the sauerkraut and one fourth of the Swiss cheese.

Microwave at high setting 2 minutes, or until cheese is melted, rotating dish one-quarter turn every 30 seconds.

Butter remaining 4 slices bread. Top each sandwich with buttered bread. Makes 4 sandwiches.

PIZZA FRANKS

1 (8-oz.) can tomato
    sauce
½ tsp. dried oregano
    leaves
⅛ tsp. dried basil leaves

6 frankfurters
6 frankfurter buns, split
4 oz. shredded pizza or
    mozzarella cheese

Combine tomato sauce, oregano and basil in bowl; mix well.

Place one frankfurter in each bun. Top each frankfurter with 2 tblsp. of the sauce.

Arrange prepared buns in 12x8x2" (2-qt.) glass baking dish. Sprinkle each with pizza cheese. Cover with waxed paper.

Microwave at high setting 3 minutes, or until cheese is melted. Makes 6 sandwiches.

HOT HAM 'N' CHEESE

4 oz. loaf-shaped
  pasteurized process
  cheese spread (like
  Velveeta)
4 English muffins, split
  and toasted
4 tblsp. Russian or
  Thousand Island salad
  dressing

1 medium tomato, cut
  into 4 slices
4 oz. sliced boiled or
  cooked ham
4 oz. sliced turkey

Cut cheese into 4 thick slices.

Spread 4 toasted muffin halves with Russian dressing, using 1 tblsp. for each. Top each with one tomato slice, one fourth of the ham and one fourth of the turkey. Place cheese slice on top.

Arrange prepared muffin halves in 12x8x2" (2-qt.) glass baking dish. Cover with waxed paper.

Microwave at high setting 2½ minutes, or until cheese is melted. Top each sandwich with a toasted muffin half. Makes 4 sandwiches.

TUNA SALAD SUBS

1 (6½-oz.) can chunk-
    style tuna, drained and
    flaked
¼ c. finely chopped celery
¼ c. finely chopped onion
½ c. mayonnaise
¼ c. sweet pickle relish

4 (6") submarine rolls,
    cut almost in half
    lengthwise
4 oz. sliced Swiss cheese
8 pimiento-stuffed olives,
    cut in half lengthwise
Lettuce leaves

Combine tuna, celery, onion, mayonnaise and pickle relish in bowl. Mix well.

Place ½ c. of the tuna mixture on bottom half of each submarine roll. Top each with Swiss cheese slices and 4 olive halves.

Place sandwiches in 12x8x2" (2-qt.) glass baking dish. Cover with waxed paper.

Microwave at high setting 4½ minutes, or until cheese is melted. Top with lettuce. Makes 4 sandwiches.

SCRAMBLED EGG SANDWICHES

8 strips bacon
½ c. chopped green
   pepper
8 eggs
¼ tsp. salt

⅛ tsp. pepper
1 (3-oz.) pkg. cream
   cheese, cut into cubes
6 frankfurter buns

Cut bacon crosswise into thin strips. Place bacon in 3-qt. glass casserole. Cover and microwave at high setting 6 minutes, or until crisp, stirring after 3 minutes.

Remove bacon and drain on paper towels. Pour off all but 2 tblsp. drippings. Add green pepper to bacon drippings in casserole. Cover and microwave at high setting 4 minutes, or until tender, stirring after 2 minutes.

Combine eggs, salt and pepper in bowl. Beat with rotary beater until blended. Add eggs and cream cheese to green pepper. Microwave at high setting 3½ to 4 minutes, stirring after every minute. (Eggs should be soft and moist at the end of cooking time as they will continue to cook on standing.) Let stand on wooden board or heatproof surface 2 minutes.

Place frankfurter buns in a circle on a plate. Cover with paper towel. Microwave at high setting 1 minute, or until warm. Split buns. Fill each bun with ⅓ c. of the egg mixture. Top with bacon strips. Makes 6 sandwiches.

MINIATURE PARTY PIZZAS

6 English muffins, split
  and toasted
1 (6-oz.) can tomato paste
2 tblsp. minced onion
2 tblsp. grated Parmesan
  cheese
¾ tsp. dried oregano
  leaves

¼ tsp. dried basil leaves
⅛ tsp. cayenne pepper
2 oz. sliced pepperoni
2 c. shredded Cheddar
  cheese (8 oz.)

Spread each toasted English muffin half with tomato paste, covering completely to edge. Sprinkle with onion, Parmesan cheese, oregano, basil and cayenne pepper. Arrange pepperoni on top and sprinkle with Cheddar cheese. Line a dinner plate with paper towels. Arrange 6 pizzas in ring on plate.

Microwave at high setting 1½ minutes, or until cheese is melted, rotating plate one-quarter turn every 30 seconds. Remove pizzas to serving platter. Repeat with remaining pizzas. Makes 12 pizzas.

CHAPTER FOUR
VEGETABLES
AND
SALADS

HOT FOUR-BEAN SALAD

6 strips bacon, diced
½ c. chopped onion
½ c. chopped green
  pepper
½ c. sugar
1 tblsp. cornstarch
⅛ tsp. pepper
¾ c. cider vinegar
1 (16-oz.) can cut green
  beans, drained

1 (16-oz.) can cut wax
  beans, drained
1 (16-oz.) can red kidney
  beans, drained
1 (16-oz.) can baby lima
  beans, drained
Dash of Tabasco sauce

Place bacon in 3-qt. glass casserole. Cover and microwave at high setting 6 minutes, or until crisp, stirring after 3 minutes.

Remove bacon and drain on paper towels. Pour off all but 1 tblsp. bacon drippings. Add onion and green pepper to bacon drippings. Cover and microwave at high setting 4 minutes, or until tender, stirring after 2 minutes.

Blend in sugar, cornstarch and pepper. Gradually stir in vinegar. Microwave at high setting 4 minutes, or until mixture thickens, stirring after 2 minutes.

Stir bacon, green beans, wax beans, kidney beans, lima beans and Tabasco sauce into vinegar mixture. Cover and microwave at high setting 8 minutes, or until hot, stirring after 4 minutes. Makes 10 servings.

BROCCOLI WITH HOLLANDAISE SAUCE

1 lb. fresh broccoli	**2 egg yolks**
¼ c. water	**1 tblsp. lemon juice**
½ c. butter or regular	**2 drops Tabasco sauce**
margarine	**⅛ tsp. salt**

Remove leaves from broccoli and cut off tough lower ends of stalks. Peel skin from lower portion of stalks. For even cooking, split each stalk in half, to 1" from floweret.

Arrange broccoli in 12x8x2" (2-qt.) glass baking dish with stalks to outside of dish and flowerets to center. Pour water over broccoli. Cover with plastic wrap, turning back one corner to allow for escape of steam. Microwave at high setting 5 minutes.

Rearrange broccoli, moving outside pieces to center. Microwave at high setting 3 to 6 minutes more, or until tender. Let stand on wooden board or heatproof surface, covered, while preparing sauce.

Place butter in 2-c. glass measuring cup. Microwave at high setting 1 minute, or until melted.

Combine egg yolks, lemon juice, Tabasco and salt in 1-qt. glass bowl; beat well. Gradually add melted butter to yolk mixture, beating with wire whisk.

Microwave at medium setting (50 percent power) 1 minute, or until sauce thickens, stirring after 30 seconds. Arrange broccoli on platter. Stir sauce and pour over broccoli. Makes 4 servings.

BUTTERED BROCCOLI SPEARS

3 lb. fresh broccoli
Butter or regular
  margarine

Salt
Pepper
Lemon slices

Remove leaves from broccoli and cut off tough lower ends of stalks. Peel skin from lower portion of stalks. For even cooking, split each stalk in half, to 1″ from floweret. Arrange stalks in cooking bag suitable for microwave ovens. Tie bag loosely with string, leaving space for steam to escape. (Do not use metal twist ties.) Microwave at high setting 6 minutes.

Turn bag over. Microwave at high setting 4 minutes more, or until tender-crisp.

Remove from bag and place in serving dish. Top with butter and season with salt and pepper. Garnish with lemon slices. Makes 6 servings.

CREAMED BRUSSELS SPROUTS

2 tsp. butter or regular
   margarine
⅓ c. fresh bread crumbs
2 (10-oz.) pkg. frozen
   Brussels sprouts
¼ c. water

1 (10¾-oz.) can
   condensed cream of
   mushroom soup
¼ c. chopped pimientos
¼ tsp. dried thyme leaves

Place butter in 1½-qt. glass casserole. Microwave at high setting 1 minute, or until melted.

Pour over bread crumbs, tossing to mix; set aside. Place frozen Brussels sprouts and water in same casserole. Cover and microwave at high setting 16 minutes, or until Brussels sprouts are tender, stirring every 5 minutes.

Drain Brussels sprouts.

Stir in mushroom soup, pimientos and thyme. Sprinkle with buttered bread crumbs. Microwave at high setting 4 minutes, or until hot. Makes 6 servings.

TANGY CABBAGE SALAD

2 tblsp. flour
2 tblsp. sugar
1 tsp. dry mustard
1 tsp. salt
$^1/_{16}$ tsp. pepper
½ c. milk
2 egg yolks, beaten
¼ c. cider vinegar
¼ tsp. celery seed

1 medium head cabbage,
   cored and shredded
   (about 5 c.)
3 medium carrots, pared
   and shredded (about
   1½ c.)
1 c. chopped green
   pepper
¼ c. minced onion

Combine flour, sugar, mustard, salt and pepper in 2-c. glass measuring cup. Gradually stir in milk. Microwave at high setting 2 minutes, or until mixture thickens, stirring every 30 seconds.

Beat egg yolks and vinegar together. Stir a small amount of hot milk mixture into yolk mixture. Immediately pour yolk mixture into remaining hot mixture, blending thoroughly. Microwave at medium setting (50 percent power) 1 minute, or until mixture thickens, stirring every 15 seconds.

Stir in celery seed. Cool to room temperature. Cover and chill in refrigerator at least 2 hours.

To serve, combine cabbage, carrots, green pepper and onion in bowl. Pour egg mixture over cabbage mixture, tossing to coat. Makes 8 servings.

GLAZED CARROTS

1½ lb. carrots, pared and
  cut into 2x¼x¹/₈"
  strips (10 medium)
1 tsp. salt
¼ c. water
3 tblsp. butter or regular
  margarine

2 tblsp. cider vinegar
2 tblsp. sugar
½ tsp. cornstarch
2 tblsp. cold water
1 tblsp. chopped fresh
  parsley

Place carrots in 2-qt. glass casserole. Dissolve salt in ¼ c. water. Pour over carrots. Cover and microwave at high setting 11 minutes, or until carrots are tender, stirring every 3 minutes.

Drain cooking liquid from carrots. Add butter, vinegar and sugar to carrots; mix lightly. Microwave at high setting 4 minutes, or until sugar dissolves, stirring after 2 minutes.

Remove carrots with slotted spoon and set aside. Blend together cornstarch and 2 tblsp. water. Stir cornstarch mixture into vinegar mixture. Microwave at high setting 1 minute, or until mixture thickens, stirring once.

Stir in carrots and parsley, tossing to mix. Makes 6 servings.

MARINATED CARROT SALAD

2 lb. carrots, pared and
 sliced (4½ c.)
½ c. water
1 onion, sliced and
 separated into rings
1 green pepper, cut into
 rings
1 (10½-oz.) can
 condensed tomato soup

2 tblsp. ketchup
½ c. sugar
½ c. vinegar
½ c. salad oil
1 tsp. salt
⅛ tsp. pepper

Place carrots and water in 2-qt. glass casserole. Cover and microwave at high setting 18 to 20 minutes, or until carrots are tender-crisp, stirring after 10 minutes.

Drain carrots. Stir onion and green pepper into carrots. Blend together tomato soup, ketchup, sugar, vinegar, oil, salt and pepper. Stir tomato soup mixture into carrot mixture. Cover and chill in refrigerator 8 hours or overnight. Makes 8 servings.

CREAMED VEGETABLE MEDLEY

1½ c. thinly sliced, pared
   carrots
2 medium onions, cut
   into eighths
6 tblsp. water
1 (10-oz.) pkg. frozen
   broccoli spears, thawed
2 tblsp. butter or regular
   margarine

2 tblsp. flour
¼ tsp. dry mustard
½ tsp. salt
⅛ tsp. pepper
1 c. milk
¼ tsp. Worcestershire
   sauce
2 tblsp. grated Parmesan
   cheese

Combine carrots, onion and water in 1½-qt. glass casserole. Cover and microwave at high setting 10 minutes, stirring after 5 minutes.

Meanwhile, cut broccoli into 1" pieces. Stir into casserole. Cover and microwave at high setting 6 minutes, or until vegetables are tender, stirring after 3 minutes.

Drain vegetables in colander. Place butter in same casserole. Microwave at high setting 1 minute, or until melted.

Blend in flour, mustard, salt and pepper. Gradually stir in milk and Worcestershire sauce. Microwave at high setting 3½ minutes, or until sauce thickens, stirring after every minute.

Stir in drained vegetables and cheese. Microwave at high setting 2 minutes, or until hot. Makes 6 servings.

CHEESY MUSTARD CAULIFLOWER

1 medium head
   cauliflower (about 2 lb.)
2 tblsp. water
½ c. mayonnaise
1 tblsp. finely chopped
   onion

1 tsp. prepared mustard
½ c. shredded Cheddar
   cheese (2 oz.)

Trim leaves from cauliflower. Leaving head whole, remove as much of core as possible by cutting a cone-shaped piece from the bottom of head.

Place cauliflower, stem side down, in 2-qt. glass casserole. Add water and cover. Microwave at high setting 12 minutes, or until tender.

Let stand on wooden board or heatproof surface 3 minutes to complete cooking. Place cauliflower on serving platter. Combine mayonnaise, onion, mustard and cheese in bowl; mix to blend. Spread mixture over cauliflower.

Microwave at medium setting (50 percent power) 1 minute. Cover with plastic wrap or waxed paper. Let stand on wooden board or heatproof surface 3 minutes, or until cheese melts. Makes 4 servings.

SWISS SCALLOPED CORN

5 tblsp. butter or regular
  margarine
½ c. buttery cracker
  crumbs (such as Ritz
  crackers)
1 c. chopped onion
½ c. chopped green
  pepper
2 (10-oz.) pkg. frozen
  whole-kernel corn,
  thawed

¾ c. evaporated milk
2 eggs, beaten
1 c. shredded Swiss
  cheese (4 oz.)
½ tsp. salt
$^1/_{16}$ tsp. pepper

Place butter in 2-qt. glass casserole. Microwave at high setting 1 minute, or until melted.

Combine 2 tblsp. of the melted butter and cracker crumbs; set aside. Add onion and green pepper to remaining butter in casserole. Cover and microwave at high setting 7 minutes, or until vegetables are tender

Stir in corn, evaporated milk, eggs, cheese, salt and pepper. Microwave at medium setting (50 percent power) 8 minutes, or until mixture thickens, stirring every 2 minutes.

Sprinkle with crumb mixture. Microwave at medium setting (50 percent power) 1 minute more. Let stand on wooden board or heatproof surface 5 minutes before serving. Makes 6 servings.

MASHED POTATO CASSEROLE

5 large baking potatoes
(2½ lb.)
1 (3-oz.) pkg. cream
cheese, cut up
1 c. milk
5 tblsp. butter or regular
margarine

1 tblsp. fresh or dried
chopped chives
¾ tsp. salt
¹/₁₆ tsp. pepper
Paprika

Wash potatoes thoroughly. Prick each potato several times with cooking fork. Arrange potatoes in ring, 1" apart, on paper towel in microwave oven. Microwave at high setting 8 minutes.

Turn potatoes over and rearrange in ring. Microwave at high setting 7 to 9 minutes more, or until tender. Let stand on wooden board or heatproof surface 5 minutes.

Peel potatoes and force through ricer. Add cream cheese, milk, 4 tblsp. of the butter, chives, salt and pepper to potatoes; mix well. Spoon potato mixture into greased 8" square glass baking dish. Dot with remaining 1 tblsp. butter and sprinkle with paprika.

Microwave at medium setting (50 percent power) 18 to 20 minutes, or until hot, rotating dish one-quarter turn every 5 minutes. Makes 6 servings.

CHEESE-STUFFED POTATOES

**6 large baking potatoes
(3 lb.)
6 strips bacon
6 tblsp. soft butter or
regular margarine
1 tsp. salt**

**⅛ tsp. pepper
1 c. milk
2 tblsp. minced onion
1½ c. shredded Cheddar
cheese (6 oz.)**

Wash potatoes thoroughly. Prick potatoes several times with cooking fork. Arrange potatoes in a ring, 1" apart, on paper towel in microwave oven. Microwave at high setting 10 minutes.

Turn potatoes over and rearrange in ring. Microwave at high setting 10 to 12 minutes more, or until tender.

Place bacon on paper towels in microwave oven. Top with additional paper towels. Microwave at high setting 5 minutes, or until crisp.

Remove bacon; crumble and set aside.

Cool potatoes slightly. Slice off top. Scoop out potatoes with spoon and place in mixing bowl. Add butter, salt, pepper, milk, onion and 1 c. of the cheese. Whip with electric mixer at medium speed until smooth. Stir in bacon. Spoon mixture back into potato shells. Arrange potatoes in a ring on serving plate. Reheat immediately or cover and refrigerate until serving time. Microwave at high setting 6 minutes, or until hot, rotating dish one-quarter turn after 3 minutes. Top with remaining ½ c. cheese. Makes 6 servings.

Note: If potatoes are refrigerated before reheating, microwave at high setting 9 minutes, or until hot, rotating dish one-quarter turn after 4½ minutes.

EASY SCALLOPED POTATOES

**4 medium all-purpose
potatoes, pared and
thinly sliced (1⅓ lb.)**
⅓ c. finely chopped onion
1 tblsp. flour
1 tsp. salt
⅛ tsp. pepper

1⅔ c. milk
**1 tblsp. butter or regular
margarine**
**½ c. shredded Cheddar
cheese (2 oz.)**
Paprika

Arrange one half of the sliced potatoes in greased 2-qt. glass casserole. Sprinkle with onion, one half of the flour, one half of the salt and one half of the pepper. Arrange remaining potatoes on top. Sprinkle with remaining flour, salt and pepper. Pour milk overall. Dot with butter.

Cover and microwave at medium setting (50 percent power) 30 minutes, or until potatoes are tender, rotating dish one-quarter turn every 8 minutes.

Sprinkle with cheese and paprika. Microwave at medium setting (50 percent power) 2 minutes, or until cheese is melted. Cover and let stand on wooden board or heatproof surface 5 minutes before serving. Makes 4 servings.

CREAMY GERMAN POTATO SALAD

**4 large all-purpose
 potatoes (about 2 lb.)
6 strips bacon, diced
½ c. chopped onion
2 tblsp. flour
2 tblsp. sugar
1½ tsp. salt**

**½ c. cider vinegar
¼ c. water
⅓ c. mayonnaise
½ tsp. celery seed
Paprika
Chopped fresh parsley**

Wash potatoes thoroughly. Prick each potato several times with cooking fork. Arrange potatoes in ring, 1″ apart, on paper towel in microwave oven. Microwave at high setting 6 minutes.

Turn potatoes over and rearrange in ring. Microwave 6 minutes more, or until tender. Let stand on wooden board or heatproof surface 10 minutes. Peel and slice potatoes; set aside.

Place bacon in 2-qt. glass casserole. Cover and microwave at high setting 5 minutes, or until crisp, stirring after 3 minutes.

Remove bacon and drain on paper towels. Pour off all but 2 tblsp. bacon drippings. Add onion to bacon drippings. Cover and microwave at high setting 2 minutes, or until tender.

Blend in flour, sugar and salt. Gradually stir in vinegar and water. Microwave at high setting 3 minutes, or until mixture thickens, stirring after every minute.

Blend in mayonnaise, celery seed and bacon. Gently fold in potatoes. Cover and microwave at high setting 4 minutes, or until hot, stirring after 2 minutes. Sprinkle with paprika and parsley. Makes 6 servings.

HOT SPINACH SALAD

**2 qt. torn spinach leaves,
stems removed (10 oz.)**
½ c. chopped onion
**1 c. halved cherry
tomatoes**
6 strips bacon, diced
2 tblsp. sugar

½ tsp. salt
¼ tsp. dry mustard
2 tblsp. lemon juice
1 tblsp. ketchup
**½ tsp. Worcestershire
sauce**

Combine spinach, onion and cherry tomato halves in salad bowl.

Place bacon in 2-qt. glass casserole. Cover and microwave at high setting 6 to 8 minutes, or until crisp, stirring every 2 minutes.

Remove bacon and drain on paper towels. Pour off all but 3 tblsp. drippings. Stir together sugar, salt and mustard in 2-c. glass measuring cup. Add lemon juice, ketchup and Worcestershire sauce to sugar mixture. Add lemon juice mixture to drippings in casserole. Microwave at high setting 1 minute, or until mixture boils.

Stir to dissolve sugar. Add bacon to spinach mixture. Pour hot dressing overall; toss well. Serve at once. Makes 6 servings.

GLAZED ACORN SQUASH RINGS

2 medium acorn squash (about 1 lb. each)
⅓ c. butter or regular margarine

¼ c. brown sugar, packed
½ tsp. ground cinnamon

Cut squash into 1" crosswise slices. Remove seeds and stringy fibers from center.

Arange slices in 12x8x2" (2-qt.) glass baking dish. Cover tightly with plastic wrap. Microwave at high setting 6 minutes.

Turn squash over and rearrange slices. Cover tightly and microwave at high setting 6 minutes more, or until tender. Drain squash.

Combine butter, brown sugar and cinnamon in 2-c. glass measuring cup; mix well. Microwave at high setting 4 minutes, or until brown sugar is dissolved.

Spoon brown sugar mixture over squash rings. Microwave squash at high setting 2 minutes. Baste squash with syrup in bottom of dish. Microwave at high setting 2 minutes more. Makes 6 servings.

BACON-STUFFED TOMATOES

6 large tomatoes
   (about 2 lb.)
¼ tsp. salt
4 strips bacon, diced
½ c. chopped onion
½ c. chopped celery
1 clove garlic, minced
2½ c. fresh bread cubes
   (½")

1 c. shredded Cheddar
   cheese (4 oz.)
2 tblsp. chopped fresh
   parsley
½ tsp. salt
⅛ tsp. pepper

Slice tops off tomatoes and discard. Scoop pulp from center with spoon, leaving ¾" thick shell. Sprinkle inside of shell with ¼ tsp. salt. Turn shells upside down and let drain. Chop pulp and drain well.

Combine bacon, onion, celery and garlic in 10" glass pie plate. Cover with waxed paper. Microwave at high setting 8 minutes, or until bacon is crisp, stirring after 4 minutes.

Combine tomato pulp, bread cubes, ¾ c. of the cheese, parsley, ½ tsp. salt and pepper in bowl. Pour bacon mixture over bread mixture, mixing well. Spoon ½ c. filling into each tomato. Arrange filled tomatoes in ring in same pie plate.

Microwave at high setting 6 minutes, or until hot, rotating dish one-quarter turn after 3 minutes. Sprinkle with remaining ¼ c. cheese. Microwave at high setting 1 minute more, or until cheese is melted. Makes 6 servings.

ZUCCHINI CUSTARD

5 c. shredded unpared
  zucchini, packed (about
  1¾ lb.)
1¼ tsp. salt
4 eggs, well beaten
1½ c. shredded Cheddar
  cheese (6 oz.)

¼ c. flour
¼ c. chopped fresh
  parsley
$1/16$ tsp. pepper

Sprinkle zucchini with salt and let stand 1 hour. Drain in colander, pressing out liquid with spoon.

Place zucchini in 8" square glass baking dish. Cover with plastic wrap, turning back one corner to allow for escape of steam. Microwave at high setting 10 minutes, stirring after 5 minutes.

Drain zucchini in colander. Dry and grease same baking dish. Combine zucchini, eggs, 1 c. of the cheese, flour, parsley and pepper in bowl; mix well. Pour into prepared dish.

Microwave at medium setting (50 percent power) 6 minutes, or until mixture thickens, stirring every 2 minutes. Sprinkle with remaining ½ c. cheese. Microwave at medium setting (50 percent power) 1 minute, or until cheese is melted. Makes 6 servings.

ZUCCHINI AND TOMATOES WITH MACARONI

1 c. chopped green
pepper
1/3 c. finely chopped onion
1 clove garlic, minced
2 tblsp. butter or regular
margarine
1 lb. unpared zucchini,
cut into 1/2" cubes
1 tsp. dried oregano
leaves

1/2 tsp. dried basil leaves
1 (28-oz.) can tomatoes,
cut up
1 c. cooked macaroni
1 beef bouillon cube
1/8 tsp. pepper
Grated Parmesan cheese

Combine green pepper, onion, garlic and butter in 2-qt. glass casserole. Microwave at high setting 4 minutes, or until tender, stirring after 2 minutes.

Stir in zucchini, oregano and basil. Cover and microwave at high setting 6 minutes, or until zucchini is tender, stirring after 3 minutes.

Stir in tomatoes, macaroni, beef bouillon cube and pepper. Cover and microwave at high setting 8 minutes, or until hot, stirring after 4 minutes. Sprinkle with cheese before serving. Makes 6 servings.

STUFFED ZUCCHINI BOATS

**2 small unpared zucchini
(¾ lb.)
2 strips bacon, diced
¼ c. chopped onion
¼ c. chopped green
pepper
1 tblsp. butter or regular
margarine**

**⅓ c. fresh bread crumbs
1 tblsp. minced fresh
parsley
1 tblsp. grated Parmesan
cheese
¼ tsp. salt
Dash of pepper
2 tblsp. water**

Cut zucchini in half lengthwise. Scoop out pulp and seeds with spoon, leaving ¼" thick walls. Chop pulp and set aside.

Place bacon in 1-qt. glass casserole. Cover and microwave at high setting 2 minutes.

Remove bacon and drain on paper towels.

Stir chopped zucchini, onion, green pepper and butter into bacon drippings. Cover and microwave at high setting 5 minutes, stirring after 3 minutes.

Drain off excess liquid. Stir in bacon, bread crumbs, parsley, cheese, salt and pepper. Set aside.

Arrange zucchini shells, cut side down, in 8" square glass baking dish. Add water to baking dish. Cover with plastic wrap, turning back one corner to allow for escape of steam. Microwave at high setting 5 minutes, or until tender, rotating dish one-quarter turn after 2 minutes.

Drain liquid from zucchini. Turn zucchini, cut side up. Spoon stuffing into zucchini shells. Microwave at high setting 1 to 2 minutes, or until heated through. Makes 4 servings.

CURRIED RICE WITH ZUCCHINI

3½ c. chopped unpared
zucchini (1 lb.)
⅓ c. minced onion
1 clove garlic, minced
2 tblsp. butter or regular
margarine
1 (10¾-oz.) can
condensed chicken
broth

1 c. uncooked regular rice
2 tblsp. chopped fresh
parsley
½ tsp. curry powder
½ tsp. salt
⅛ tsp. pepper
1¼ c. very hot tap water

Combine zucchini, onion, garlic and butter in 3-qt. glass casserole. Cover and microwave at high setting 4 minutes, stirring after 2 minutes.

Stir chicken broth, uncooked rice, parsley, curry powder, salt, pepper and hot water into zucchini mixture. Cover and microwave at high setting 20 minutes, or until rice is tender, stirring every 7 minutes. Makes 6 servings.

CHAPTER FIVE

GREAT COUNTRY DESSERTS

OLD-FASHIONED CARROT CAKE

1½ c. sifted flour
2½ tsp. ground cinnamon
1¼ tsp. baking soda
¾ tsp. salt
1½ c. sugar
1 c. cooking oil
1 tsp. vanilla

3 eggs
2½ c. finely grated, pared
  carrots
½ c. raisins
½ c. chopped walnuts
Cream Cheese Frosting
  (recipe follows)

Sift together flour, cinnamon, baking soda and salt; set aside.

Combine sugar, cooking oil and vanilla in bowl. Beat until well blended, using electric mixer at medium speed. Add eggs, one at a time, beating well after each addition.

Add dry ingredients, carrots, raisins and walnuts to sugar mixture, stirring to blend well. Pour mixture into greased 12x8x2" (2- qt.) glass baking dish.

Microwave at high setting 12 to 13 minutes, or until top springs back when touched lightly with finger, rotating dish one-quarter turn every 3 minutes. Cool in dish on wooden board or heatproof surface.

Prepare Cream Cheese Frosting. Frost cake with Cream Cheese Frosting. Makes 16 servings.

Cream Cheese Frosting: Beat together 1 (3-oz.) pkg. cream cheese (softened), 3 tblsp. butter or regular margarine and 1 tsp. vanilla in bowl until smooth, using electric mixer at medium speed. Gradually add 2 c. sifted confectioners' sugar; beat until smooth and creamy, using electric mixer at low speed.

SPICY APPLESAUCE CAKE

1 c. raisins	1 c. sugar
½ c. water	1 egg
1 c. applesauce	1 tsp. vanilla
1½ c. sifted flour	½ c. chopped walnuts
1 tsp. baking soda	Lemon Icing (recipe
½ tsp. ground cinnamon	follows)
⅛ tsp. ground cloves	
½ c. butter or regular margarine	

Combine raisins and water in 2-c. glass measuring cup. Microwave at high setting 3 minutes, or until mixture comes to a boil. Stir in applesauce. Cool to lukewarm.

Grease 2½-qt. glass mixing bowl. Place greased 2½" diameter drinking glass in center of bowl; set aside.

Sift together flour, baking soda, cinnamon and cloves; set aside.

Cream together butter and sugar in bowl until light and fluffy, using electric mixer at medium speed. Beat in egg and vanilla.

Add dry ingredients alternately with applesauce mixture to creamed mixture, beating well after each addition. Stir in walnuts. Turn mixture into prepared bowl.

Microwave at high setting 8 minutes, or until cake tester or wooden pick inserted in center of cake comes out clean, rotating dish one-quarter turn after 4 minutes. (Top of cake will be moist.) Cool in bowl on wooden board or heatproof surface 10 minutes. Remove cake from bowl. Cool on rack.

Prepare Lemon Icing. Drizzle cake with Lemon Icing. Makes 10 servings.

Lemon Icing: Combine 1¾ c. sifted confectioners' sugar, ⅛ tsp. grated lemon rind, 2 tblsp. lemon juice and 1 drop yellow food coloring in bowl. Beat until smooth, using a spoon.

COCONUT-TOPPED OATMEAL CAKE

1 c. quick-cooking oats	1 c. brown sugar, packed
1½ c. water	½ c. sugar
1⅓ c. sifted flour	2 eggs
1 tsp. baking soda	1½ tsp. vanilla
1 tsp. ground cinnamon	Caramel-Coconut
½ tsp. salt	Topping (recipe
¼ tsp. ground nutmeg	follows)
½ c. butter or regular	
margarine	

Combine oats and water in 1½-qt. glass casserole. Microwave at high setting 3 minutes, or until mixture thickens, stirring after 2 minutes. Set aside.

Sift together flour, baking soda, cinnamon, salt and nutmeg; set aside.

Cream together butter, brown sugar and sugar in bowl until light and fluffy, using electric mixer at medium speed. Add eggs, one at a time, beating well after each addition. Blend in vanilla. Stir in oat mixture.

Gradually add dry ingredients to creamed mixture, beating well after each addition, using electric mixer at low speed. Turn mixture into 12x8x2" (2-qt.) glass baking dish.

Microwave at high setting 11 minutes, or until cake tester or wooden pick inserted in center comes out clean, rotating dish one-quarter turn every 3 minutes. Cool in dish on wooden board or heatproof surface.

Prepare Caramel-Coconut Topping. Spread Caramel-Coconut Topping over warm cake. Serve warm. Makes 12 servings.

Caramel-Coconut Topping: Combine 1 c. flaked coconut, ½ c. chopped walnuts, ½ c. brown sugar (packed), ½ c. milk, ¼ c. butter or regular margarine and dash of salt in 1-qt. glass casserole. Microwave at high setting 6 minutes, or until mixture is thick and bubbly, stirring every 2 minutes.

LEMON-GLAZED GINGERBREAD RING

1½ c. sifted flour
¾ tsp. ground ginger
¾ tsp. ground cinnamon
½ tsp. baking powder
½ tsp. baking soda
½ tsp. salt
½ tsp. ground nutmeg
¼ tsp. ground cloves

½ c. cooking oil
½ c. brown sugar, packed
½ c. molasses
½ c. boiling water
2 eggs
Lemon Glaze
  (recipe follows)

Grease 2-qt. glass casserole. Place greased 2" diameter drinking glass in center of casserole; set aside.

Sift together flour, ginger, cinnamon, baking powder, baking soda, salt, nutmeg and cloves; set aside.

Beat together oil, brown sugar, molasses and boiling water in bowl until brown sugar is dissolved, using electric mixer at medium speed. Add eggs, one at a time, beating well after each addition.

Gradually add dry ingredients to molasses mixture, beating well after each addition, using electric mixer at low speed. Pour batter into prepared casserole.

Microwave at medium setting (50 percent power) 12 minutes, or until cake tester inserted in center comes out clean, rotating dish one-quarter turn after 6 minutes. Cool in dish on wooden board or heatproof surface 10 minutes. Unmold. Cool on rack.

Prepare Lemon Glaze. Drizzle cake with Lemon Glaze. Makes 10 servings.

Lemon Glaze: Combine 1½ c. sifted confectioners' sugar, 2 tblsp. lemon juice, ½ tsp. grated lemon rind and 1 drop yellow food coloring in bowl. Stir until smooth.

HURRY-UP BROWNIES

1 c. sifted flour
½ tsp. baking powder
½ tsp. salt
½ c. butter or regular
   margarine
2 (1-oz.) squares
   unsweetened chocolate

1 c. sugar
2 eggs
1 tsp. vanilla
½ c. chopped walnuts

Sift together flour, baking powder and salt; set aside.

Place butter and chocolate in 8″ square glass baking dish. Microwave at medium setting (50 percent power) 3 minutes, or until melted.

Stir in sugar. Add eggs and vanilla, beating well. Gradually stir dry ingredients into chocolate mixture, blending well. Stir in walnuts.

Microwave at high setting 5 minutes, or until top is no longer wet, rotating dish one-quarter turn every 2 minutes. Cool in dish on wooden board or heatproof surface. Cut into 2″ squares. Makes 16.

CHOCOLATE CHIP BARS

1¼ c. sifted flour
½ tsp. baking powder
½ tsp. salt
½ c. butter or regular
  margarine
⅓ c. sugar

⅓ c. brown sugar, packed
1 egg
1 tsp. vanilla
1 (6-oz.) pkg. semisweet
  chocolate pieces

Sift together flour, baking powder and salt; set aside.

Cream together butter, sugar and brown sugar in bowl until light and fluffy, using electric mixer at medium speed. Add egg and vanilla, beating well.

Gradually stir dry ingredients into creamed mixture, blending well. Stir in ⅔ c. of the chocolate pieces. Spread mixture in 8" square glass baking dish.

Microwave at high setting 4 minutes, or until a wooden pick inserted in center comes out clean, rotating dish one-quarter turn every 1½ minutes. Cool in dish on wooden board or heatproof surface.

Place remaining chocolate pieces in 1-cup glass measuring cup. Microwave at medium setting (50 percent power) 2 minutes, or until melted, stirring after 1 minute. Spread chocolate over bars. Cool until chocolate is set. Cut into 2x1" bars. Makes 32.

FROSTED MOLASSES SQUARES

1½ c. sifted flour
1½ tsp. baking powder
1 tsp. ground cinnamon
½ tsp. salt
¼ tsp. baking soda
¼ tsp. ground cloves
½ c. shortening

½ c. sugar
1 egg
½ c. light molasses
½ c. water
Confectioners' Sugar
  Icing (recipe follows)

Sift together flour, baking powder, cinnamon, salt, baking soda and cloves; set aside.

Cream together shortening and sugar in bowl until light and fluffy, using electric mixer at medium speed. Add egg, beating well. Blend in molasses and water.

Gradually stir dry ingredients into creamed mixture, blending well. Spread in greased 12x8x2" (2-qt.) glass baking dish.

Microwave at high setting 7 minutes, or until a wooden pick inserted in center comes out clean, rotating dish one-quarter turn every 2 minutes. Cool in dish on wooden board or heatproof surface.

Prepare Confectioners' Sugar Icing. Frost bars with Confectioners' Sugar Icing. Cut into 2" squares. Makes 24.

Confectioners' Sugar Icing: Combine 1½ c. sifted confectioners' sugar, 5 tsp. milk and ½ tsp. vanilla in bowl. Beat until smooth, using a spoon.

CHEESECAKE BARS

⅓ c. butter or regular
    margarine
⅓ c. brown sugar, packed
1 c. sifted flour
½ c. chopped walnuts
1 (8-oz.) pkg. cream
    cheese, softened

¼ c. sugar
1 egg
1 tblsp. milk
1 tblsp. lemon juice
½ tsp. vanilla

Cream together butter and brown sugar in bowl until light and fluffy, using electric mixer at medium speed. Stir in flour and walnuts. (Mixture will be crumbly.) Remove 1 c. crumb mixture and reserve for topping. Press remaining crumb mixture into bottom of 8" square glass baking dish.

Microwave at high setting 2 minutes, rotating dish one-quarter turn after 1 minute.

Beat cream cheese in bowl until smooth, using electric mixer at medium speed. Gradually add sugar, egg, milk, lemon juice and vanilla, beating well. Spread cream cheese mixture over crust. Sprinkle with reserved 1 c. crumb mixture.

Microwave at high setting 6 minutes, or until set, rotating dish one-quarter turn every 2 minutes. Cool in dish on wooden board or heatproof surface. Cut into 2" squares. Makes 16.

THUMBPRINT COOKIES

2 c. sifted flour
¼ tsp. salt
1 c. butter or regular
   margarine
½ c. brown sugar, packed

2 egg yolks
½ tsp. vanilla
1¼ c. finely chopped
   walnuts
½ c. red currant jelly

Sift together flour and salt; set aside.

Cream together butter and brown sugar in bowl until light and fluffy, using electric mixer at medium speed. Add egg yolks and vanilla, beating well.

Gradually stir dry ingredients into creamed mixture, blending well. Shape mixture into 1" balls. Roll balls in walnuts. Arrange 7 balls in ring, equally spaced, on 10" round of cardboard covered with waxed paper. Place cardboard in microwave oven on an inverted saucer.

Microwave at high setting 45 seconds.

Press thumb into center of each ball, making an indentation. Rotate one-quarter turn. Microwave 55 seconds more, or until dry on surface. Slide waxed paper from cardboard to wooden board or heatproof surface. When cool, place 1 heaping measuring teaspoon currant jelly in indentation in each cookie. Makes 3½ dozen.

PEANUT BUTTER COOKIES

1½ c. sifted flour
¼ tsp. baking soda
¼ tsp. salt
½ c. shortening
½ c. peanut butter

½ c. sugar
½ c. brown sugar, packed
1 egg
1 tsp. vanilla

Sift together flour, baking soda and salt; set aside.

Cream together shortening, peanut butter, sugar and brown sugar in bowl until light and fluffy, using electric mixer at medium speed. Add egg and vanilla, beating well.

Gradually stir dry ingredients into creamed mixture, blending well. Shape mixture into 1" balls. Arrange 6 balls in ring, equally spaced, on 10" round of cardboard covered with waxed paper. Flatten each with a fork, making a crisscross pattern. Place cardboard in microwave oven on an inverted saucer.

Microwave at high setting 1 minute 15 seconds, or until dry on surface, rotating cardboard one-quarter turn after 40 seconds. Slide waxed paper from cardboard to wooden board or heatproof surface. Cool. Makes 3 dozen.

CHOCOLATE SCOTCHEROOS

6 c. toasted rice cereal
1 c. sugar
1 c. light corn syrup
1 c. peanut butter
1 (6-oz.) pkg. semisweet
chocolate pieces

1 (6-oz.) pkg.
butterscotch-flavored
pieces

Arrange cereal in greased 13x9x2" (3-qt.) glass baking dish. Set aside.

Combine sugar and corn syrup in 3-qt. glass casserole. Microwave at high setting 4 minutes, or until mixture boils, stirring after 2 minutes.

Add peanut butter and stir until melted. Pour mixture over cereal. Cool in dish on wooden board or heatproof surface.

Combine chocolate pieces and butterscotch-flavored pieces in 1-qt. glass casserole. Microwave at high setting 2 minutes, or until melted, stirring after 1 minute. Spread over cooled bars. Cool completely. Cut into 1½" squares. Makes 48.

ROCKY ROAD CHOCOLATE PIE

¼ c. butter or regular
  margarine
1¼ c. graham cracker
  crumbs
2 tblsp. sugar
1 (6-oz.) pkg. semisweet
  chocolate pieces
½ c. milk
2 c. miniature
  marshmallows

¼ c. toasted sliced
  almonds
1 (1½-oz.) env. whipped
  topping mix
½ c. milk
½ tsp. vanilla
Sweetened whipped
  cream
1 (1-oz.)square semisweet
  chocolate, grated

Place butter in 9″ glass pie plate. Microwave at high setting 1 minute, or until melted. Stir in graham cracker crumbs and sugar; mix well. Press crumb mixture into bottom and up sides of same pie plate.

Microwave at high setting 1½ minutes, rotating dish one-quarter turn after 45 seconds. Cool on rack.

Combine chocolate pieces and ½ c. milk in 2-c. glass measuring cup. Microwave at high setting 3 minutes, or until chocolate is melted, stirring after 2 minutes. Pour mixture into metal bowl. Stir until smooth. Add marshmallows and almonds, stirring just until coated. Cover and chill in refrigerator 30 minutes.

Prepare whipped topping mix with ½ c. milk and vanilla according to package directions. Fold whipped topping into chocolate mixture. Turn into graham cracker crust. Cover and freeze until firm.

Before serving, spoon puffs of sweetened whipped cream around edge of pie. Sprinkle with grated chocolate. Makes 6 to 8 servings.

COCONUT CREAM FLOATING ISLANDS

½ c. sugar
3 tblsp. cornstarch
⅛ tsp. salt
3½ c. milk
2 drops yellow food
  coloring

2 egg yolks, beaten
½ c. flaked coconut
1 tsp. vanilla
2 egg whites
¼ c. sugar
Ground cinnamon

Combine ½ c. sugar, cornstarch and salt in 2-qt. glass casserole. Gradually stir in milk and food coloring.

Microwave at high setting 4 minutes. Stir well. Microwave at high setting 4 minutes more, or until mixture comes to a boil and thickens, stirring after every minute.

Stir a small amount of hot mixture into egg yolks. Immediately pour yolk mixture back into remaining hot mixture, blending thoroughly. Microwave at high setting 30 seconds. Stir in coconut and vanilla. Cool to room temperature.

Pour into 6 individual serving dishes. Cover and chill in refrigerator at least 2 hours.

Meanwhile, beat egg whites in bowl until foamy, using electric mixer at high speed. Gradually add ¼ c. sugar, 1 tblsp. at a time, beating well after each addition. Continue beating until stiff, glossy peaks form when beaters are slowly lifted. Place a sheet of brown wrapping paper on baking sheet. Drop mixture in 6 mounds, in ring on brown paper. Slide paper from baking sheet to floor of microwave oven.

Microwave at high setting 1 minute, or until meringues are set. Slide paper back onto baking sheet. Cool meringues on baking sheet.

To serve, place one meringue on each serving. Sprinkle each with cinnamon. Makes 6 servings.

CREAMY RICE PUDDING

¾ c. sugar
2 tblsp. cornstarch
¼ tsp. salt
2 c. milk
2 egg yolks, beaten

2 c. cooked regular rice
1 tblsp. butter or regular
   margarine
1 tsp. vanilla
Ground nutmeg

Combine sugar, cornstarch and salt in 1½-qt. glass casserole. Gradually stir in milk. Microwave at high setting 8 minutes, or until mixture comes to a boil and thickens, stirring every 2 minutes.

Stir a small amount of hot mixture into egg yolks. Immediately pour yolk mixture back into remaining hot mixture, blending thoroughly.

Microwave at high setting 2 minutes, stirring after 1 minute. Fold in rice, butter and vanilla. Cover with plastic wrap and chill in refrigerator. Sprinkle with nutmeg. Makes 6 servings.

FUDGE PUDDING CAKE

1 c. sifted flour
3 tblsp. baking cocoa
1 tsp. baking powder
½ tsp. salt
2 tblsp. butter or regular
   margarine
½ c. sugar
1 tsp. vanilla

½ c. milk
½ c. chopped pecans
½ c. sugar
5 tblsp. baking cocoa
¼ tsp. salt
1⅔ c. boiling water
Confectioners' sugar
Vanilla ice cream

Sift together flour, 3 tblsp. cocoa, baking powder and ½ tsp. salt; set aside.

Place butter in glass bowl. Microwave at high setting 1 minute, or until melted. Stir in ½ c. sugar and vanilla; blend well.

Add dry ingredients alternately with milk to sugar mixture, beating well after each addition, using a spoon. Stir in pecans.

Combine ½ c. sugar, 5 tblsp. cocoa, ¼ tsp. salt and boiling water in 8" square glass baking dish; mix well. Drop batter by rounded teaspoonfuls into liquid.

Microwave at high setting 8 minutes, or until top springs back when touched lightly with finger, rotating dish one-quarter turn after 4 minutes. Sprinkle with confectioners' sugar. Serve warm with ice cream. Makes 8 servings.

RASPBERRY CHEESECAKE ROYALE

¼ c. butter or regular
   margarine
1¼ c. graham cracker
   crumbs
4 (3-oz.) pkg. cream
   cheese, softened
¾ c. sugar

2 eggs
1 tsp. vanilla
1 c. dairy sour cream
3 tblsp. sugar
½ tsp. vanilla
Red Raspberry Sauce
   (recipe follows)

Place butter in 8″ round glass baking dish. Microwave at high setting 1 minute, or until melted. Stir in graham cracker crumbs and mix well. Press crumb mixture into bottom and 1″ up sides of same baking dish.

Cream together cream cheese and ¾ c. sugar in bowl, using electric mixer at medium speed. Add eggs, one at a time, beating well after each addition. Blend in 1 tsp. vanilla. Pour mixture into graham cracker crust.

Microwave at medium setting (50 percent power) 12 minutes, or until center is almost set, rotating dish one-quarter turn every 3 minutes. Remove from microwave oven; let stand 5 minutes.

Combine sour cream, 3 tblsp. sugar and ½ tsp. vanilla in bowl and mix well. Spread mixture over cheesecake.

Microwave at medium setting (50 percent power) 2 to 3 minutes, or until top is set. Cool on rack. When cooled, cover and chill in refrigerator at least 3 hours before serving.

Prepare Red Raspberry Sauce and serve with cheesecake. Makes 8 servings.

Red Raspberry Sauce: Thaw 1 (10-oz.) pkg. frozen red raspberries. Drain raspberries in sieve, reserving juice. Add enough water to juice to make ¾ c. liquid. Combine 2 tblsp. sugar and 1 tblsp. cornstarch in 2-c. glass measuring cup; mix well. Stir in ¾ c. reserved juice and 1 tsp. lemon juice. Microwave at high setting 2 minutes 15 seconds, or until thickened, stirring every 45 seconds. Stir in raspberries. Cool completely.

SPICY APPLE CRISP

**6 c. thinly sliced, pared
  tart apples**
¼ c. chopped pecans
¼ c. raisins
⅔ c. brown sugar, packed
⅓ c. unsifted flour
⅓ c. quick-cooking oats

½ tsp. ground cinnamon
¼ tsp. ground nutmeg
**3 tblsp. butter or regular
  margarine**
**Sweetened whipped
  cream**

Combine apples, pecans and raisins in bowl. Arrange one half of the apple mixture in 9″ glass pie plate. Sprinkle with ⅓ c. of the brown sugar. Top with remaining apple mixture.

Combine remaining ⅓ c. brown sugar, flour, oats, cinnamon and nutmeg in bowl. Cut in butter until mixture is crumbly, using pastry blender. Sprinkle crumb mixture over apple mixture.

Microwave at high setting 10 minutes, or until apples are tender, rotating dish one-quarter turn every 4 minutes. Spoon into dessert dishes. Top with whipped cream. Makes 6 servings.

ORANGE-COCONUT APPLE CRISP

6 c. sliced, pared tart
apples
2 tblsp. orange juice
⅔ c. brown sugar, packed
⅓ c. unsifted flour
½ tsp. grated orange rind

⅓ c. butter or regular
margarine
1 c. flaked coconut
Sweetened whipped
cream

Arrange apples in 8″ square glass baking dish. Sprinkle with orange juice.

Combine brown sugar, flour and orange rind in bowl. Cut in butter until mixture is crumbly, using pastry blender. Add coconut and toss to mix. Sprinkle brown sugar mixture over apples.

Microwave at high setting 12 minutes, or until apples are tender, rotating dish one-half turn after 6 minutes. Cool slightly. Spoon into dessert dishes. Top with whipped cream. Makes 6 servings.

APPLE-CRANBERRY DESSERT

3 c. sliced, pared tart
  apples
2 c. fresh or frozen
  cranberries
1 c. sugar
1 tblsp. lemon juice
¼ tsp. salt

1 c. brown sugar, packed
1 c. quick-cooking oats
½ c. unsifted flour
⅓ c. butter or regular
  margarine
Sweetened whipped
  cream

Combine apples, cranberries, sugar, lemon juice and salt in bowl; mix well. Turn into 8″ square glass baking dish.

Combine brown sugar, oats and flour in bowl. Cut in butter until crumbly, using a pastry blender. Sprinkle crumb mixture over apple mixture.

Microwave at high setting 9 minutes, or until apples are tender, rotating dish one-quarter turn after 5 minutes. Let stand on wooden board or heatproof surface 45 minutes before serving. Spoon into dessert dishes. Top with whipped cream. Makes 6 servings.

EASY CHERRY CRISP

1 (24-oz.) jar cherry pie
   filling
½ (18½-oz.) pkg. yellow
   cake mix
¼ c. butter or regular
   margarine

¼ c. finely chopped
   walnuts
2 tblsp. brown sugar,
   packed
1 tsp. ground cinnamon
Vanilla ice cream

Arrange cherry pie filling in 8" square glass baking dish. Sprinkle with cake mix and dot with butter.

Combine walnuts, brown sugar and cinnamon in bowl. Sprinkle over top.

Microwave at high setting 10 minutes, rotating dish one-quarter turn every 3 minutes. Serve warm with ice cream. Makes 6 servings.

PEACH MELBA CRISP

⅓ c. sugar
3 tblsp. cornstarch
1 (10-oz.) pkg. frozen
  raspberries, thawed
4 c. sliced, pared peaches
  (5 medium)
1 c. quick-cooking oats

¾ c. unsifted flour
¾ c. brown sugar, packed
½ tsp. ground cinnamon
¼ tsp. salt
½ c. butter or regular
  margarine, melted

Combine sugar and cornstarch in 8″ square glass baking dish. Stir in raspberries. Microwave at high setting 6 minutes, or until mixture is thickened and translucent, stirring every 2 minutes. Stir in peaches.

Combine oats, flour, brown sugar, cinnamon, salt and melted butter; mix until crumbly. Sprinkle over peach mixture.

Microwave at high setting 10 minutes, or until peaches are tender, rotating dish one-quarter turn after 5 minutes. Makes 6 servings.

PEACH CRUMBLE

**2 (29-oz.) cans sliced
  peaches, drained
¾ c. unsifted flour
½ c. sugar**

**½ tsp. ground cinnamon
½ c. butter or regular
  margarine
Vanilla ice cream**

Arrange peach slices in 9″ glass pie plate. Microwave at high setting 3 minutes, or until hot.

Combine flour, sugar and cinnamon in bowl. Cut in butter until mixture is crumbly, using pastry blender. Sprinkle over hot peaches.

Microwave at high setting 2 minutes. Serve warm with ice cream. Makes 8 servings.

STRAWBERRY-RHUBARB CRISP

2 lb. fresh rhubarb
1 (3-oz.) pkg. strawberry-
    flavored gelatin
1 tblsp. cornstarch
½ c. unsifted flour

½ c. sugar
½ c. brown sugar, packed
½ tsp. ground cinnamon
¼ c. butter or regular
    margarine

Wash rhubarb; cut off and discard leaves. Cut rhubarb stalks into ¾" pieces. You will need 5 c. diced rhubarb. Arrange rhubarb in 8" square glass baking dish.

Combine strawberry gelatin powder and cornstarch in bowl. Sprinkle over rhubarb.

Combine flour, sugar, brown sugar and cinnamon in bowl. Place butter in glass measuring cup. Microwave butter at high setting 1 minute, or until melted. Stir butter into flour mixture and mix until crumbly. Sprinkle over rhubarb.

Microwave at high setting 9 minutes, or until rhubarb is tender, rotating dish one-quarter turn after 4 minutes. Let stand on wooden board or heatproof surface 30 minutes before serving. Makes 6 servings.

PEARS IN ORANGE SAUCE

1½ c. sugar
1¼ c. water
¼ c. orange juice
1 tblsp. lemon juice
½ tsp. grated orange rind

⅛ tsp. salt
2 tsp. vanilla
6 Anjou pears, pared,
  halved and cored
  (2½ lb.)

Combine sugar, water, orange juice, lemon juice, orange rind, salt and vanilla in 3-qt. glass casserole. Cover and microwave at high setting 6 minutes, or until mixture boils.

Add pear halves. Cover and microwave at high setting 14 minutes, or until pears are tender, stirring after 7 minutes. Cool to room temperature. Cover and chill in refrigerator at least 2 hours before serving. Makes 6 servings.

SEAFOAM CANDY

1 ½ c. brown sugar,
    packed
1 c. sugar
½ c. light corn syrup
½ c. water

⅛ tsp. salt
2 egg whites
1 tsp. vanilla
½ c. chopped walnuts

Combine brown sugar, sugar, corn syrup, water and salt in 3-qt. glass casserole. Microwave at high setting 5 minutes. Stir well. Microwave 9 minutes more, or until mixture reaches 260° (hard ball stage).

Beat egg whites with vanilla in bowl until soft peaks form, using electric mixer at high speed. Slowly pour hot syrup over egg whites, beating until mixture holds its shape and begins to lose its gloss. (Mixture will be stiff.) Fold in walnuts. Working quickly, drop mixture by teaspoonfuls onto waxed paper-lined baking sheets. Makes 1 ¼ lb.

PECAN CRUNCH

1 c. sugar
½ c. light corn syrup
⅛ tsp. salt
1 c. pecan halves

1 tblsp. butter or regular
   margarine
1 tsp. vanilla
1 tsp. baking soda

Combine sugar, corn syrup and salt in 1½-qt. glass casserole. Microwave at high setting 4 minutes.

Stir in pecans. Microwave at high setting 4 minutes, or until lightly browned, stirring after 2 minutes.

Stir in butter, vanilla and baking soda, mixing well. Pour mixture onto greased baking sheet, spreading as thin as possible with metal spatula. When candy begins to set, loosen from baking sheets. Stretch and pull candy as thin as possible, using two forks. When completely cooled, break into pieces. Makes 1 lb.

CARAMEL POPCORN BALLS

2 qt. warm popped corn
1 c. sugar
2 tblsp. light corn syrup
½ c. water

1 tblsp. butter or regular
  margarine
1 tsp. baking soda

Spread freshly popped corn in large roasting pan. Keep warm in 250° conventional oven.

Combine sugar, corn syrup and water in 4-c. glass measuring cup. Microwave at high setting 5 minutes, stirring every 2 minutes. Microwave at high setting 6 minutes more, without stirring, or until golden. Stir in butter and baking soda, mixing well.

Pour hot syrup over warm popped corn, stirring to coat. Shape mixture into 1¾" balls, using about ⅓ c. for each ball. Place on waxed paper-lined baking sheets and let cool. Makes 24.

CHOCOLATE PECAN FUDGE

½ c. butter or regular
  margarine
1 (16-oz.) box
  confectioners' sugar
½ c. baking cocoa

¼ c. milk
1½ c. miniature
  marshmallows
½ c. chopped pecans
1 tsp. vanilla

Place butter in 2-qt. glass casserole. Microwave at high setting 1 minute, or until melted.

Add confectioners' sugar, cocoa and milk, blending well. Microwave at high setting 2 minutes. Stir chocolate mixture with spoon to blend.

Add marshmallows, pecans and vanilla, stirring until marshmallows are melted and blended into chocolate mixture. Pour into buttered 8″ square baking pan. Cover and chill in refrigerator until set. Cut into 1″ squares. Makes 1¾ lb.

MARSHMALLOW FUDGE SAUCE

1 (4-oz.) pkg. German   **¼ c. milk**
sweet chocolate, cut up
2 c. miniature
marshmallows

Combine chocolate, marshmallows and milk in 1½-qt. glass casserole.

Microwave at high setting 1½ to 2 minutes, or until chocolate is melted and marshmallows are soft. Stir until marshmallows melt and mixture is blended. Serve warm over ice cream or cake. Makes 1 c.

BUTTER BRICKLE ICE CREAM SAUCE

1½ c. sugar
1 c. evaporated milk
¼ c. light corn syrup
¼ c. butter or regular
  margarine

1 (7.8-oz.) pkg. almond
  brickle chips

Combine sugar, evaporated milk, corn syrup and butter in 1½-qt. glass casserole. Microwave at high setting 6 minutes, stirring every 2 minutes.

Stir almond brickle chips into syrup. (Sauce is thin, but will thicken on standing.) Cool sauce to room temperature, stirring occasionally. Serve over ice cream. Makes 2½ c.

PEANUT BUTTER ICE CREAM SAUCE

1 ¼ c. brown sugar,
   packed
⅔ c. light corn syrup
¼ c. butter or regular
   margarine

¼ tsp. salt
1 c. creamy peanut butter
1 (5.3-oz.) can evaporated
   milk (⅔ c.)

Combine brown sugar, corn syrup, butter and salt in 1½-qt. glass casserole. Microwave at high setting 4 minutes, or until mixture boils, stirring after 2 minutes.

Add peanut butter, stirring until mixture is smooth. Stir in evaporated milk. Serve warm over ice cream. Makes 3 c.

Note: Store any leftover sauce in refrigerator. To reheat sauce, place desired amount in measuring cup. Microwave at medium setting (50 percent power) 1 to 2 minutes, or until hot. Do not boil.

INDEX

A

Acorn Squash Rings, Glazed, 77
Apple
  -Cranberry Dessert, 102
  Crisp, Orange-Coconut, 101
  Crisp, Spicy, 100
Applesauce Cake, Spicy, 85
Asparagus Luncheon Roll-Ups, 37

B

Bacon and Egg Scramble, 38
Bacon-Stuffed Tomatoes, 78
Barbecued Beef Sandwiches, 53
Barbecued Meat Loaf, 20
Bean Salad, Hot Four-, 62
Beef
  Ground
    Barbecued Meat Loaf, 20
    Crustless Hamburger Pizza, 19
    Easy Vegetable Soup, 46
    Enchilada Casserole, 15
    Garden Vegetable Dinner, 14
    Meatball Stroganoff, 21
    Mexican Taco Casserole, 18
    Monte Vista Tamale Pie, 16
    and Noodles, Italian-Seasoned, 12
    Oriental Hamburger with Pea Pods, 13
    -Potato Casserole, Layered, 10
    Potato-Topped Hamburger Dinner, 11
    Quick and Easy Chili, 17
    Sandwiches, Barbecued, 53
    Swedish Meatballs, 22
    Sweet 'n' Sour Meatballs, 23
    Taco Burgers, 54

Microwave Reuben Sandwiches, 55
Pot Roast in Gravy, 8
  with Vegetables, Chinese, 9
Broccoli with Hollandaise Sauce, 63
Broccoli Spears, Buttered, 64
Brownies, Hurry-Up, 88
Brussels Sprouts, Creamed, 65
Busy-Day Spinach Soup, 49
Butter Brickle Ice Cream Sauce, 113
Buttered Broccoli Spears, 64

C

Cabbage Salad, Tangy, 66
Cake(s)
  Coconut-Topped Oatmeal, 86
  Lemon-Glazed Gingerbread Ring, 87
  Old-Fashioned Carrot, 84
  Spicy Applesauce, 85
Canadian Cheese Soup, 58
Candy(ies)
  Caramel Popcorn Balls, 110
  Chocolate Pecan Fudge, 111
  Pecan Crunch, 109
  Seafoam, 108
Caramel-Coconut Topping, 86
Caramel Popcorn Balls, 110
Carrot(s)
  Cake, Old-Fashioned, 84
  Glazed, 67
  Salad, Marinated, 68
Casserole(s)
  Company-Style Tuna, 35
  Enchilada, 15
  Garden Vegetable Dinner, 14
  Italian-Seasoned Beef and Noodles, 12

115

F

G

H

I

L

M

S

T

V

EMPLOYEE
BOOK SALE

NOT TO BE
RESOLD